Australian former professional basketball player, Lauren Jackson was only fifteen years old when she made the Australian under-20 team and one year later, found herself playing for The Opals. Her statistics are extraordinary. She's represented Australia in four Olympics winning three silver medals, won a world championship and spent twelve seasons with the Seattle Storm where she was the first foreigner to be crowned Most Valuable Player. Since retiring in 2016 she has continued her involvement with the game as assistant general manager and board member of the Deakin Melbourne Boomers.

MY STORY

MY STORY

LAUREN JACKSON

With FREDA MARNIE NICHOLLS

ALLEN&UNWIN

SYDNEY·MELBOURNE·AUCKLAND·LONDON

First published in 2018

Copyright © Lauren Jackson 2018

Allen & Unwin
83 Alexander Street
Crows Nest NSW 2065
Australia
Phone: (61 2) 8425 0100
Email: info@allenandunwin.com
Web: www.allenandunwin.com

 A catalogue record for this book is available from the National Library of Australia

ISBN 978 1 76029 487 8

Set in 12/17.5pt Sabon by Midland Typesetters, Australia
Printed and bound in Australia by Griffin Press

10 9 8 7 6 5 4 3 2 1

The paper in this book is FSC® certified. FSC® promotes environmentally responsible, socially beneficial and economically viable management of the world's forests.

Contents

Foreword

I have spent most of my lifetime in the game of basketball. First as a player, a three-time Olympian for the United States, and then coaching at university, professional and international levels. I took the head coaching job with the Seattle Storm in 2003, familiar with the sweet All-American perception of Seattle player Sue Bird, as well as the perceived brash and edgy, but brilliant Aussie by the name of Lauren Jackson. Lauren's reputation preceded her, punctuated by plenty of technical fouls and stories of run-ins with our American star, Lisa Leslie. Honestly, on that first day, I had no idea how our relationship would develop. I certainly didn't imagine just how deep and caring our bond would become and evolve over the years.

I remember clearly the first time I walked into the gym where LJ was working out with our assistant coaches. I had watched Lauren carefully through the years, from when she played as a 16 year old with her national team, as well as too many times on the opposing bench. She was a star in the WNBA, and at a very young age had established herself as a force in women's basketball. I expected to meet a cocky, outspoken player but was stunned instead to meet a young woman who struggled to hold eye contact or exude anything remotely boastful. In that first court workout I affirmed what I *did* know about Lauren—she was a star. Her skill set was unique and her versatility was unparalleled. I could see her passion and commitment to getting better. I knew then, that we could achieve something special, but that's Lauren's story to tell.

Coaching the greatness that is Lauren Jackson is one of the most significant times in my career. Working with a GOAT (Greatest Of All Time) level player is the ultimate dream that every coach hopes for. These elite athletes have unmatched physical gifts of course, but it is their drive and work ethic that separates them from their peers. Lauren's drive to be the best was the force that propelled her to the top.

In this memoir, Lauren lets the reader into her journey. As I read it, it was as if I was with her at so many critical stages of her life. Lauren has had to overcome many trials and make very difficult decisions regarding her health, career and personal life. In this book, you will get to know Lauren, the person. You will see her strength, determination and unwavering toughness. You will be amazed at what she endured to win all those titles, awards and medals of greatness.

I believe in the old adage that sometimes 'our greatest strength can be our biggest weakness'. In Lauren's case, this was certainly true. LJ's commitment to excellence and the internal ambition to excel, blinded her from taking care of her health. Her pain tolerance and inclination to ignore her body's warning signals, caught up with LJ both physically and emotionally. In this book, Lauren details her struggles and the implausible choices that she made in order to compete. It also forces the rest of us involved in her career, to examine our own inclination to look past those same warning signs, and to go along with Lauren in her determination to simply, play on.

By reading this fascinating autobiography, you will have a better understanding of Lauren's complex personality. She opens up about her extraordinary family and the unbreakable bond that she shares with her parents. The relationship and support of her family throughout her life, has enabled Lauren to spread her wings and explore basketball and cultures all over the world. Readers will get to see that a basketballer's life can be full of experiences that are both glamorous and gruelling.

In reading Lauren's memoir, you will walk through the unfinished life of one of Australia's greatest treasures. You will experience the joy that she has found after retiring from basketball at only 35 years of age. You will discover that this legend is experiencing a love surpassing all others. I couldn't be more proud of this beautiful woman and count my blessings that our paths have crossed.

Anne Donovan
2008 USA Olympic Basketball Coach
2004 Seattle Storm Championship Coach
Wilmington, NC
(1 November 1961–13 June 2018)

Anne wrote this foreword a month or two before we finished the book. With her sudden passing I feel so fortunate that she not only had the chance to read the book, but that she had the opportunity and agreed to write this foreword. She passed away on 13 June 2018 from heart failure, and I, too, feel truly blessed that our paths crossed. I send love and care to her family and all those who loved her.

Lauren Jackson

1

∎ ∎ ∎

Standing Tall

I was probably born to play basketball because of my height, my parents' influence and being around a court from when I can first remember—but what talent I had isn't something that can be belted into kids, it's an ability, and it still took time and dedication to achieve success.

In any professional sport, especially a contact sport like basketball, you need to be able to hold your own, you need to be tough, but I certainly didn't start out that way. From the time of my earliest memories, my parents inspired me as professional basketball players in their own right, and my mum is still the first person I turn to whenever I have questions, or if I have issues going on in my life. We have a beautiful mother–daughter relationship. I trust her, and that is a big thing for me. Having Mum around always filled me with confidence when I was younger, and still does. As a child, I was a bit of a 'mummy's girl'—awkward, uncertain—but I was also incredibly strong-willed. Poor Mum, she had to help me get through all of that.

The more I grew, the more I played, the higher up in competition I went, that tough style of play eventually began to come naturally on the court—it became who I was, it defined me. If I felt intimidated when I played, instead of showing it I would turn it into aggression. That was always what the public saw—the confident basketballer, my determination, skill and aggression on court. But I know there is a real dichotomy to my personality.

When people get to know me, they often ask me why I'm shy. I'd say I'm more reserved than shy. I was definitely shy when I was younger, but now I think I'm just wary, it takes a lot for me to trust, and until I get to that point I tend to shut people out. From the time I was a child, whenever something was going on in my life that I struggled with, I would simply shut it out and move on, and that's how I tended to handle a lot of things. I'm sure that some people saw that sort of behaviour as aloof or stand-offish, but it's a coping mechanism I've carried with me my entire life. It's certainly how I dealt with being tall.

Growing up in the regional city of Albury, in southern New South Wales, I learnt from a young age that when you look different, people stare, however rude it is. When people see me, I reckon a lot of them instantly think 'Wow, she's tall!', and they'll stop and gawk. I just became oblivious to that from a really early age. As a result, today I can go down the street and not notice people, I'll walk along and not even see them. People who don't know me often misconstrue that as me being rude, but it's just how I've always dealt with it, because I've been so tall my entire life. It's just easier to shut it out and pretend it's not happening.

Height is definitely in my genes. Mum and Dad are both tall. Mum is 1.88 metres (6 feet 2 inches) and Dad 1.95 metres (6 feet 5 inches), and at 1.96 metres (6 feet 6 inches) I stand a good centimetre taller than Dad. Dad tells a funny story about the time I had a health check at primary school. The school nurse sent a note home, asking to see my parents because she was concerned about my size and height, and mentioning the possible need for some health checks to be carried out. Mum and Dad walked into the school, and as soon as they met the nurse she took one look at them and apologised, she could see where I got my height from. Dad and I butted heads when I was growing up, well and truly. He has a tough exterior, but he's also sensitive, and probably too soft with me and my mum. I've always known that I could call Dad about anything and he would be the first one to help me, he's my strongest advocate and friend.

I thought we had a fairly traditional family dynamic, with Dad being the tough one, Mum the softer parent, but it wasn't until I was much older that I realised Mum is the glue, *she* is the tough one who holds us all together. Everybody who knows her just loves her, she doesn't bitch or complain, she just goes and does what needs to be done. I don't think I've ever respected anyone enough for them to replace her, or Dad, in my life.

Both my parents played representative basketball for Australia. Dad played both the shooting guard position and the small forward position or number 3, predominantly a 3man. In a basketball game, there are five players from a team on the court at a time: two guards (numbers 1 and 2), a centre (number 5) and two forwards (numbers 3 and 4). The shooting guard or 2 tends to be taller than the point guard, and is good at long-range three-point shots taken outside the key (the key shape on the court extending around the basket), as well as helping set up shots for other players. My childhood hero Michael Jordan was an amazing 2man. Small forward was the position Dad played most for Australia, having the versatility of long-range shooting, but also having the strength and agility to get into the key and drive to the basket.

Mum was a centre, or post player, playing close to the hoop, or basket—the 5 is a tall player who can take shots around the rim while handling the physicality that happens in the key. She was a truly formidable player in her time, incredibly tall and strong for a female basketballer. Mum also grew up in Albury, and one of her old coaches, Charlie Leaney, would pick her up at 5.30 am for training during the week at the local basketball courts (which back then were inside the poultry pavilion at the local showground), before dropping her home again to get ready for work. In 1973, at the age of 18, she was selected to play basketball for the Australian women's national basketball team, who would eventually be known as the Opals. Mum met Dad in 1974 at a national basketball championship in Sydney that she was playing in. I always find it so moving when they tell their love story, it's really beautiful.

Mum went on and played in the 1975 International Basketball Federation (FIBA) World Championship for Women in Colombia, South America, where the Australian team came tenth in the world. The FIBA World Championship is a huge competition involving nations from all over the world—it's held once every four years, and together with the Olympics, is the most important championships in women's basketball. In 1977, Mum became one of the first Australian women to gain an American college basketball scholarship, playing for Louisiana State University from 1977 to 1979. She played in the 1979 FIBA World Championship for Women, when the national team improved Australia's ranking, coming in fourth. Mum travelled with the Opals to Bulgaria in 1980 to play in a pre-Olympic tournament, but they didn't qualify, losing to the US and Hungary in their round.

In 1975, Dad was playing for the men's national team, the Boomers, and was known as a really athletic basketballer. He toured the US and China with the national team, and Mum jokes that the first thing she fell in love with about him was his jump shot—when I see photos of my dad from back then he was such a handsome man, with a great body. My parents were madly in love, and they married in Albury in 1977. While Mum was playing in the US, they kept in touch with a phone call once a week and voice letters on tapes, until Dad joined her after his basketball commitments with the City of Sydney team were finished. When Mum returned to Australia in 1979, they settled in Albury and built a home there in the suburb of Thurgoona. I came along in May 1981, a 9 pound 10 ounce (4.4 kilogram) baby girl, with Mum back playing for Albury and coaching basketball just two weeks after giving birth to me naturally, which I still find incredible. When my parents were travelling by bus to Mum's first game after having me, sitting up the front with me as a newborn, the bus driver ran into the back of a car. We obviously all survived and everything was fine, but Mum still says that it was pretty scary at the time, given she was a new mum and holding me in her arms when it happened. She still talks about that.

My brother Ross was born 14 months after me. We both have very strong personalities. Everything I say annoys him one way or the other, but that's just our sibling relationship. He's been there for me through some of my hardest times, he's done his best to support me, and as much as we fight and carry on, Ross is the true definition of a brother, he's my mate. His passion has always been trains, and when he left school he became a signalman and became the rail safety and operations manager for Transport Heritage NSW, and is still working for a company in rail operations. He loves the work and is really good at it, which just goes to show that if you're passionate about what you do, you can succeed. My passion has always been basketball, and I'd never change my passion for the world—but a passion like his that will last him the rest of his life, that's pretty cool.

Ross and I literally grew up in and around basketball stadiums, with Mum back on the Australian team in 1982 just months after my brother was born. Australia needed to beat New Zealand in a three-game Oceania series in Melbourne on their path to qualify for the 1984 Olympics. My maternal grandmother, Nanna Bennie, travelled down with Mum to Melbourne, while Dad looked after me and Ross, with the help of his parents, back in Albury. Australia won the series, but on the trip home Mum announced to Nan that she didn't want to travel or be away from us. She'd decided that enough was enough, and she called it a day on her Australian career. She was 29, back in shape and playing well, but there was a long European tour coming up with the Opals, and she felt she couldn't leave us. Looking back now I find that a pretty amazing thing to do. The Australian women's basketball team ended up coming fifth at the Los Angeles Olympic Games in 1984, the men's team managed seventh.

Mum kept playing locally, still dominating in her games. Even though she was no longer representing Australia, she and Dad kept travelling and playing in competitions, always taking us with them. Ross and I spent countless hours exploring and playing inside basketball stadiums as toddlers and little kids, even sleeping under the bleachers (the raised seating alongside the court) when we were tired. At two years of age I apparently told my aunt that I was also going to play basketball for Australia. A pretty bold statement for a little kid, but basketball was already my life. My parents were so special in my eyes, still are, they were both incredible basketball players, and if they'd played for Australia, so could I. I didn't want to do or be anything else.

We were the sporty family, and my mum was the super-sporty mum. I always enjoyed playing basketball from my first memories of it, always felt at home on the court. I could be a determined little bugger at times as well. I remember thinking that I should have been on court with the adults, even though I was just a little kid and not even playing in competitions. But I truly believed I would be able to play better than all the adults I was watching, if I could just get out there and prove it. I eventually started playing in kids' competitions when I was about five or six years of age, and again I thought I was better than I actually was—because I really wasn't that good. I don't know why I felt this way, because I could be a bit of a sook as a kid, but I also had a tendency at that age to be too big for my own boots.

I know Mum found my attitude pretty hard to take, and to add to that dynamic she then became my basketball coach. Whenever she was around I felt invincible, but when she wasn't I became the biggest weakling in the world. Mum decided to teach me how to be tough on the court, how to harden up and not be so soft. The feeling that she didn't think much of me was really upsetting, so I put even more effort into toughening up my game.

I played my very first representative game for Albury when I was about ten, and we had to travel three hours down to

Melbourne. I don't remember what happened exactly, but apparently I hit someone on the court and the referee threw me out of the stadium. They kicked me out of Albert Park Stadium in Melbourne, a ten-year-old kid with no supervision, and left me standing outside. That must have been so embarrassing for Mum. I remember her telling me afterwards that with behaviour like that I would never represent Australia, and I was completely heartbroken. Because of my parents and who they were in basketball, particularly in Albury, I think I felt entitled. It was a sense of entitlement that I didn't deserve, but I still had dreams. I was a bit of a brat, I had real attitude.

I was about 11 years old when I first played representative school basketball. My school team went to the Riverina regional trials, but Mum couldn't take time off work for the trip, and without her there I wasn't so invincible. I missed out on selection for the Riverina representative team and another girl from school made it through. I was completely shattered. Missing out certainly lowered my confidence, and I started to doubt myself, to think I wasn't good enough— I have fought this feeling within myself throughout my career, and it has always pushed me to work harder. Missing out was probably the best thing that could have happened to me at the time, because it helped to keep my attitude— which was obviously pretty bad at that point—in check.

I broke my foot when I was about 12, stupidly kicking out at my brother in anger. It was Boxing Day and we were in Sydney with Dad's family, Ross was being a smart aleck about something silly, and my uncle was in the background egging us on. I got fed up and lashed out at Ross and hit his hip bone with my foot. I saw him about to cry and felt bad, and then a split second later I realised I'd hurt myself, and that felt much worse. Mum thought I was lying about the pain, probably thought I was trying to get out of trouble, so initially she didn't do anything about the injury. Three hours later she looked at my foot and it was the size of a football, and she took me to the hospital to have it seen to. Funnily enough, a few years later I did the same thing, kicked Ross in almost the same place, and broke the same bone again. I don't kick him anymore, he'd probably just sit on me now anyway.

After that first bone break and Mum thinking I was lying, I was a total mess. I was a bit hysterical, I was in so much pain and I couldn't walk on it. Mum's opinion meant the world to me, and she hadn't believed a word I'd said, but I think that also made me toughen up. Physically I can work through most pain—although that turned out to be detrimental to me later in my career, because I would always play through injuries.

2

...

Toughening Up

Dad set up a basketball court at home, a quarter court, and we'd play 'two on two', one adult and child against the other two, something we continued to do for many years. It was pretty physical. Dad, and then Ross as he got older, could be competitive, and I had to step up if I was going to get any points. I'd practise on that court every day, even by myself, shooting the ball at the basket, shooting hoops. I wanted to be a guard like my Dad—I can shoot like him—but I also wanted to be strong for my size like my Mum. I think I got the best of both of my parents' respective basketball skills, and Mum and Dad helped me train, but they didn't box me into one category as a basketballer, or as a person. Dad didn't tell me to focus on my three-point shots outside the key, Mum didn't say I only needed to learn how to do a turnaround jump shot (jumping and turning in the air to shoot) or insist that I prioritise my inside game. I had to learn how to do it all, and I did. They let me explore basketball as I developed, do what I wanted to do, and it paid off. Because of my height, I started off playing in teams in the centre position, where you need to be tall and strong to tap the ball away from the opposing centre in the jump-off at the start of the game. A centre also needs to be able to take the hits, to be tough.

When I was growing up, we watched US National Basketball Association (NBA), men's basketball, it was the only basketball shown on television here at the time, and as a result I really admired American players like Michael Jordan. When you watch a NBA championship it's amazing, the players are so athletic. Today, players like LeBron James are huge and strong, and physically just superior athletes in comparison with probably everybody. It's magic watching them, run, dunk, play—for me it's truly beautiful. Women basketballers aren't usually as big as men, so are easier to shut down on court, compared with having someone like LeBron James flying over your head. There are some girls who are particularly tall and strong, but women's basketball is a different game from men's, it's more about strategy and skill, and tends to be a much more tactical game as a result. As our coach, Mum was helping me and the other girls in our Albury under 12s team understand this, while at home I'd be playing against the physically stronger men in our family, trying to toughen up on both fronts.

Mum was still our coach when I started high school. We'd train at the courts in the Albury Sports Stadium—which had been built a couple of years after I was born to replace the old courts in the poultry pavilion—and we'd play there most weekends. I knew that place so well, I truly grew up there. Most of the time at training we would be practising our plays, both offensive (attacking or engaging the other team) and defensive (trying to stop the other team scoring), as well as improving the accuracy of our shooting and generally just handling the ball. I would practise shooting, especially from the free-throw line, near the top of the key, over and over. I'd spin the ball in my hand as I looked up at the basket, gather myself, control my breathing, imagine the ball going through the hoop, sense how it would feel, and then, finally, take the shot. I came to know the weight of the ball, the feel of its tough seamed surface, I knew how it would pass through the air, knew how it would feel when I caught it. I would bounce it in front of me as I walked along the road to training, until that hard, perfect ball became a part of me, an extension of myself.

When I was in year 7, my first year at Murray High School, someone asked me what I wanted to be when I left school. I told them that I would only stay at Murray High until year 10, then I would go on to the Australian Institute of Sport (AIS), and after that I was going to play basketball for Australia. I definitely said it, and truly believed it. I wasn't even that good a basketballer back then, I'd missed out on teams, but I knew that was the pathway for me if I was going to be a professional basketball player.

My first two years at Murray High were tough. I hated school because I couldn't learn in an environment where I had kids around me constantly, where I was surrounded by talking, activity. I couldn't concentrate, I was just all over the place. It would be many years until I found a way to learn that suited me. In order to learn—whether that be a textbook or a basketball play—I must have what I need in front of me, with nothing else going on nearby, no distractions. I had difficulties learning the traditional way and I still find myself getting easily distracted. As a result, I was put in the lower classes at high school. I wasn't completely hopeless, I managed to be an average student, but it wasn't the best learning environment for me. If I could have been doing anything other than study, I would have.

From the age of about 11, I'd shot up in height. I'd always been taller than other girls, but by the time I was at Murray High I was heading towards 1.8 metres (6 feet) and struggled with being openly teased about it. In a lot of my adult basketball stats I'm described as 1.96 metres (6 feet 5 inches), but that's wrong. In the US, they add inches, here I took one off. I didn't want people to think I was as tall as I actually was, I truly thought that removing that extra inch would somehow make me more acceptable. Even now I think my height can be intimidating to others. I can certainly feel overwhelmed and awkward when I'm around people taller than I am, so I can only imagine how shorter people feel around me.

Being so much taller than everyone else at high school, I 'shut down' and tried to ignore stares and comments. I felt awkward and out of place. I got called names, lots of names, about anything—my height, even the whole girl thing. I was called a slut, which the boys thought was an acceptable thing to say to girls, and I even remember being called gay, which back then was considered probably the worst slur for a boy or a girl. I'm not sure we even knew what it meant, just that it was used as an insult. It's so insignificant now, but I remember being in that moment, being tormented, feeling shame and anger.

I was struggling, but I would never have considered opening up to Mum and Dad, I didn't want to appear weak, and so coped in my own way. I always arrived at school on an early bus, and as a result I was isolated from my friends. Being so young and tall, I was an easy target. When we pulled up at school, I'd get off the bus and go and sit in the toilets and hide, waiting until my friends arrived— I didn't want to hear or deal with any hurtful remarks. I had some teachers who probably knew I was struggling, one in particular, Mrs Crossley, was my roll call and English teacher. Every day that I walked into her class I felt better just seeing her, I felt that someone was there for me. But at one stage she became ill and missed a bit of school, and I really missed seeing her, and her gentle presence until she returned.

Being in a classroom was the worst part of my day, but when I was home or on my way to the basketball stadium, I was fine. I think my parents knew something was going on, growing up they would have had to deal with the same sort of remarks about being tall themselves. I also think that's why my parents encouraged me to play basketball, they knew I had trouble fitting in, even though I didn't talk about it.

I don't think the bullying I went through was any worse than what others suffered, but the way I ended up responding to it was. I would come home and self-harm, cutting my arms, legs, whatever I could reach. I couldn't block out the bullying and how it was making me feel, so I think I was finding a physical outlet by cutting myself, doing something to hurt myself. I still have the scars, and that's where I have some of my tattoos, I tried to cover the marks—I only did it a few times, the scars aren't terrible. I think for my parents, reading something like this will be upsetting, but it's not their fault. I hid it from them, I certainly didn't tell them. I'm not saying this to make them feel bad at all, it was just a part of my life and a part of my story that helped shape me, it doesn't define me by any means. When we're young I think we do whatever we can to cope, because we don't have the emotional tools to deal with the way we're feeling.

In retrospect, my high school years were the hardest of my life. But even though I would never wish to go back and relive that time, it made me who I am. I just had to get through that period, and once I'd done that, it was over. The bullying eventually stopped completely, it was a phase. The minute I found my place, which was playing basketball, I was accepted and I was fine. Now I'd say to kids going through that stage in life, find an outlet, play sport as much as you can, even if you don't think you're good enough, find a physical outlet.

I continued not to react at school to the bullying, but then one morning I did. This guy was teasing me, calling me names, I can't even remember what names, but I walked over to him and physically pushed him away, and got into him. I was just a girl responding to a name, but I was so angry, I remember thinking, 'Can you just let me get through this morning without saying something, anything!' It wasn't just him, it was that time, not being able to find my identity, not being accepted for who I was, that was brutal. Those early high school years are your formative years, you don't know how to deal with your emotions, you don't know how to compartmentalise, you don't know anything, you just try and live and figure it out day by day. People ask me now how I compartmentalise so well—it's easy, it's how I've lived my life. If I've struggled with anything, I've been able to put it into a box, and then go and play basketball at my best, and that's how I ultimately dealt with the bullying, that's the lesson I took forward from that time. I feel so sorry for teenagers who are subjected to bullying, and especially today with smart phones, they can never escape it. For me back then, my home and basketball were my escape.

My ultimate reaction to the bullying was to become harder, although it didn't stop the bullies from bullying. It made me tougher, angrier, as I always felt like I was being attacked. I became rebellious, and my parents responded by taking me out of school sport at Murray High. I was only allowed to play basketball for Albury. I used to watch the sport presentations at the end of each school year and feel

I should have been getting those awards and sporting blues, so I guess it was pretty good punishment. I also think it gave my parents a bit of relief, in the sense that if they'd allowed me to play school sport I would have been doing every team sport available to me at the time. It was certainly getting to that point prior to Mum and Dad putting their foot down.

I loved playing basketball so much that I was out on our court at home mucking around and shooting whenever I had spare time. It felt great to be good at something. I wasn't always trying to improve my game, I just loved doing it. Mum and Dad were still good players back then, Mum had a beautiful shot, she could consistently knock down baskets from outside the key, so even when I thought I was better than her, she'd simply knock down a three-pointer. She was really smooth like that, and so was Dad. Basketball was probably the only thing I truly cared about outside my parents and my family. Basketball made me feel like I belonged.

3

. . .

Mission Statement

When it was announced back in September 1993 that Sydney was going to host the 2000 Olympic Games I was 12 years old, and I remember telling Mum, 'I'm going to be there!'. Mum looked straight at me, and from her expression, it felt to me like she was thinking, 'You can't even get through training without crying'. I didn't care, nothing was going to deter me, it was something I was going to achieve. Credit to my parents, as much trouble as I put them through, they never said that it wasn't going to happen—it was always doable, *everything* was doable.

Mum was coach for the Albury under-12s, as well as for the under-14s during my first year at high school, when I began playing with two girls who would become my closest friends, Brodey Ball and Chelsea Grant. Brodey was at Murray with me, but she was popular, and we didn't become friends until year 9 when my life at high school started to turn around. My friends were a sanctuary for me and aside from the occasional school yard drama, were my closest mates. Looking back, Brodey and I had a funny dynamic, she was one of the cool girls and I wasn't, or I didn't feel I was. In my first couple of years at Murray High we couldn't stand each other, didn't even acknowledge each other's existence, even though we'd been playing basketball together since we were about five years old. By year 9 we'd started playing representative basketball together, and after that we'd sit on the big tree trunk in the middle of the school yard during lesson breaks and talk all the time. We grew up together. Brodey is such a beautiful person, it's funny how you understand and appreciate the importance of these close friendships as you grow older.

I progressed from Albury to the NSW Country under-14s team, and played in the Australian Country Junior Tournament held in Albury the following January. Junior basketball teams come to Albury annually from all over the country, and that year my team made it to the final. During the final, my knee started hurting—it wasn't too bad, I could have kept playing. I went off the court (I think we were already losing) and into the training room and wanted someone to fix my knee, but they couldn't, so I just didn't go back out there. Dad came into the first aid room and told me to get back on the court, but my knee hurt, and it was all too hard.

We lost that finals match, and I thought my parents were mad at me because they felt I'd let my team down. I remember Mum saying to me, 'Lauren, if you don't want to play, you don't have to, but you do not ever let your teammates down'. I remember that so vividly. She went on, telling me that she and Dad weren't going to push me to play, there was no obligation, I didn't have to play to make them love me, they would love me no matter what, but I could not let my teammates down in a situation like that again. Ever. It was at that moment I realised just how much my behaviour had affected my parents. They thought I was only playing basketball to make them happy, they clearly thought my heart and soul weren't in it at that point, and they wanted to give me the opportunity to get out if I didn't want to be there. I think they were embarrassed more than anything, they thought I felt pressured to play, but I didn't, I loved it, there was just a part of me that continued to act like a spoilt brat who thought she was better than the rest. I only ever wanted them to be proud of me—but I didn't understand what that meant until they *weren't*. That's when I realised I couldn't continue to act that way. From that moment, I gained more self-awareness and more awareness of people around me, I started becoming a better basketballer really, maybe a better person too.

When we arrived home after the tournament, I went straight into the computer room, wrote my version of a mission statement, and printed it out. My Dad's best friend and his family were staying with us and I was a bit embarrassed that they were privy to the whole thing, but mostly I felt bad that Mum thought I was a bit of a sook and I had clearly let her down. The spelling was atrocious and definitely came from a 12 year old, but in my mission statement I said that I wanted to play basketball because I loved it, and that I wouldn't be a big bag of wuss anymore. When I read it years later I remember thinking, 'Oh my god, do you really need to show people this?'. I have been notoriously private my whole life, so even the littlest things impact me. You don't want people knowing your vulnerabilities I guess, and I felt that was one of mine.

Writing that damn mission statement was a turning point for me. I'd made a commitment, whether I knew it or not, to harden up, toughen up and, perhaps more importantly, to be accountable. I trained, no one told me to, there was just something in me that made me work harder. I didn't wake up and think 'Today I'm going to train', it was just in the back of my mind. No matter what, at some point in the day I would pick up a basketball and practise—wherever I went, I had a basketball in my hands, I wouldn't put it down. That was my life from then on, I was always around a basketball court and if I wanted to achieve my dream, that was what I had to do.

I started making teams. Once I started being selected, I had an obligation to train, I knew I had to work harder to stay there. I was chosen to go on the NSW intensive training centre program in Sydney and Terrigal on the Central Coast for elite young kids in the state, and they gave me goal-setting tasks and shooting drills that I had to do every night. I was being held accountable and I took it on, I was going to succeed. I wasn't fanatical, I wasn't the sort of kid who would practise a thousand shots a day, but when I did train, I trained relentlessly. Everything started happening after that.

After the previous year's debacle of not going back on court at the Country Junior Tournament, it was personally satisfying when my under-14s NSW Country team won the 1995 championship. It was a great fun game in my home town. Winning that was awesome. I then went on to play on several NSW Country and NSW State teams over the next year, and at the age of just 13, I was invited to play for the national junior team, the Gems. The junior team was for players under 20 years, the senior team, the Opals, is for the best players in Australia and has no age limit.

When good things happened, instead of getting excited I tended to get anxious. I was excited but I was also scared that it was too good to be true, that it could all go away, it would disappear—but I guess I never took anything for granted as a result. I did always worry about everything and, looking back, I wish I could have done that better, I wish I could have just enjoyed moments rather than being anxious about the future all the time.

4

■ ■ ■

Gems

Before each tournament, the national junior and senior teams always held training and team selection camps, usually at the AIS in Canberra. These camps were great for building team chemistry, especially when the majority of us didn't play together on a regular basis, or didn't know the coach. Going to that first training camp with the Gems was when my basketball career really took off. Looking back now, 13 is so young for all of that to happen.

At that first camp, I was really nervous, I truly felt out of my league, like I didn't belong. I was the youngest there. The rest of my team were aged between 15 and 17, so the others at the camp were at least two, three or even four years older than me, which is a big difference at that age. Teenage girls can be cruel, but I was also a socially awkward kid, I didn't know how to fit in, and I missed the security of having Mum around. When Mum had been coaching, she was always at home games and at most away games, but now she couldn't take time off work and travel with me to Canberra, and I was really missing her. My whole life I'd felt that I'd been picked on, or laughed at, or bullied. Although not so much in the Albury basketball teams, with Mum as our coach—I eventually made great friends in those teams, but at the start it was hard. Being tall and awkward in junior high school and being the youngest in the Gems, that wasn't a lot of fun.

I was scared, but I was also thrilled to be there. At that first camp, I didn't know anybody on the squad and I kept to myself, especially after pulling my hamstring on the second day. To my surprise, at the end of the training camp it was announced that I'd made the team to go to the US later that year. I was so excited, and all I wanted to do was ring Mum and Dad to tell them. I was a kid, and kids didn't generally have a mobile phone back then, so I had to find a payphone to call them, and eventually spotted one in a building at the AIS. There were a group of girls from the Gems camp standing near this payphone, and as they saw me walking towards them they ran off to go and hide from me, making it obvious that they didn't want to be around me. Two of the popular girls at the camp hadn't been chosen to go the US, and I think they were mad at me because I'd made the team and they hadn't. Although it was ridiculous looking back on it now, it affected me nonetheless. I hated the way

I felt at that time—I wasn't good at socialising, but I guess I just wanted to be liked. Back then, I was too busy trying to fit in when in hindsight I should have just been myself.

I travelled with the team to Texas in May 1995, and turned 14 over there. It was my first time overseas, I missed home and missed Mum even more on my birthday. The Gems played 11 tournament games against different teams over a fortnight, a pretty demanding schedule. We played against college players aged between 18 and 24, and there were some pretty big-name players in the other teams, girls who would go on to play for the US Women's National Basketball Association (WNBA). I didn't play all the games, I wasn't what's known as a 'starter' then, someone in the starting line-up of players. They're usually the best players on the team at their respective positions, and consequently there's a bit of prestige associated with being a starter. I was the youngest and most inexperienced in the team, and ended up playing only five of those 11 games. Basketball Australia saw it as a trip to initiate us all into the US style of game, and were hoping at best for a 6–5 win/loss record. The Gems won nine of those 11 games.

When we returned to Australia, the AIS offered me a scholarship to attend the following year and Mum and Dad said no straight away. They felt that at 14, I was just too immature. If they'd asked me, I would have done it in a heartbeat, but they were right, it took me that year to try and get used to the idea of being away from them, away from Mum.

On my next overseas trip with the Gems, something happened that would plague me for the rest of my life. We flew to Taiwan and played the R. William Jones Cup against senior teams from around the world. The Gems played against three teams from the host country Taiwan, as well as teams from both North and South Korea, Thailand, Japan, Slovakia and the US, and won seven of the nine games. We came in third behind the US and Slovakia, which everyone was stoked about, and the team were upbeat as we drove to the airport to head back home.

I didn't have many close friends on the team at that stage, I was still pretty much a loner. Three or four hours into the flight home, my teammates were doing their own thing, I remember some of them were playing cards, talking among themselves, and I moved to the back of the plane where there was an empty row so I could stretch out and have a sleep. I've always been the type of person who imagines the worst, and for some reason as I slept I dreamt that the plane was crashing. I woke in a panic to find we were flying through heavy turbulence, and I just started freaking out. I felt I couldn't breathe, and I was crying hysterically—I was having a full-blown anxiety attack. No one I knew was around me and I couldn't understand what was happening, I truly thought we were about to crash. When the turbulence stopped and I realised we weren't falling out of the sky, I just sat there and sobbed, trying to get my breathing under control and settle myself down. It had been a dream, but it had seemed so real,

I'd seen it happening! From then on, I would always have problems with flying.

I do always think the worst. I have a really good way of talking myself into disaster in my head, and I would regularly dream of crashing when I slept on planes. In those early years, I would often cry myself to sleep during a flight, have a dream and wake up feeling even worse. I would get so worked up before having to travel on a plane that I'd often make myself sick. I did speak to someone later at the AIS about my anxiety attacks on planes and they suggested meditation, but that certainly didn't work. They suggested I imagine myself in my favourite place in the world—which was Mum and Dad's house, home—and that just made me worse. Imagine myself on a beach? Why? I didn't want to be on a beach, I wanted to be with the people I loved. I was very stubborn. There were episodes where I'd work myself into such a state that I would cry for almost the entire trip, trying all the while to hide it from my older teammates. That fear was one of the major things I battled with during my career, and as I progressed in my sport, the flying became never ending.

I didn't tell anyone when that first attack happened. I didn't want my teammates to find out because I was embarrassed, I didn't want to show I was vulnerable and give anyone another reason to laugh at me.

■ ■ ■

It was decided that I would take up the AIS scholarship in 1997 at the start of year 11. 1996 was to be my last year at Murray High, and Mum and Dad finally let me play basketball for the school. I was already representing Australia in the national junior team, and they let me go to the NSW State Championships with Murray. We won, which was a huge achievement for a small country school, and we were then invited to the Australian School Championships to be held in Canberra. Half the school drove up to Canberra to watch us compete in the final at the AIS, and I played well, or I think I did, I think I was top scorer.

Just before going to the high school nationals I'd kicked my brother that second time and managed to break the same bone in my foot. Ross and I were so competitive. If we were playing one on one in the backyard he'd start dunking, and I'd retaliate, telling him he didn't even like the sport and here he was dunking on me! Dunking is very common in the men's game, when they get to the rim and literally grab the iron when releasing the ball into the hoop. (At that stage I don't know if any woman had ever done that in a professional game.) My brother had gone from being an uncoordinated boy with no athletic traits whatsoever, someone who didn't like sport, to become the strongest kid around. Physically, he was powerful, he stood at 2.03 metres (6 feet 8 inches), he could jump, and his body was doing all the things I wished mine would do. I was still treating him like he was my annoying little brother, and he was able to pick me up and throw me in the pool if he wanted. In frustration, I'd stupidly kicked out at him, and broken my toe, again. I hadn't gone to hospital, we'd just left it, and my toe was really swollen before the finals. I already knew the physiotherapists at the championships from attending training camps at the AIS, so I went to see them and they made me a plaster cast that wrapped around my shoe, in case anyone trod on my foot. I played the entire tournament wearing that cast. It was ugly but it was worth it, we won! Murray was the best high school basketball team in Australia that year.

Things had settled down at Murray High. People were nicer to my face, I had my group of friends and it wasn't as torturous as those first years—and then to win the school championship in my last year there was such an awesome moment. Going back to school with our medals, the shield and trophy, and standing in front of all the students with the team, it was great. I felt like I was on a cloud, and at the end of year 10 I was awarded a sporting blue. After getting through such a rough few years at high school, being presented with a sporting blue was probably the single proudest moment of my entire school career.

5

...

Australian Institute of Sport

The move to the AIS was pivotal in my life. I missed my mum and dad terribly, but I was lucky compared with some of the other school-age kids, my parents were only four hours down the road instead of on the other side of the continent.

Mum and Dad drove me to Canberra and dropped me at the institute and left, and it wasn't until years later Dad told me that Mum cried all the way home. I've never seen her cry and I've never seen her take a sick day either, but she apparently had to take the following day off work after they left me at the AIS at the start of 1997. Mum and I are so close, but I needed to be away from home, because if I'd stayed I think I would have never left, never have grown up.

Mum told me later that she was just as scared as I was. I know it was hard for both her and Dad. They made an effort to be there for me, making a point of coming up every second weekend, they didn't just leave me there, I never felt abandoned. The AIS had started in 1981, the same year that I was born, so it hadn't been around when my parents were playing. I don't remember getting any advice from them, it was more a matter of them just telling me to embrace it. I don't think they knew what to expect either.

I was still pretty young, and stood at about 1.93 metres (6 feet 4 inches). Even though I was taller and bigger than the other girls, it didn't bother me, because I felt like I finally belonged. I was living with all these other athletes from all over the country and felt completely at home. I fitted in, I felt normal and it was the first time I ever felt like that in my entire life, other than being with my family.

At the AIS, routine kicked in. If I was in camp with the Gems, we would have two to two-and-a-half-hour training sessions a day, Thursday through to Sunday. During the weekends, we'd normally be playing in competition, and during the week I'd have two or three individual training sessions with a coach, and also train every afternoon with the AIS development team (but did manage to have Wednesday afternoons off). We also had shooting practice—I had to get 100 shots in a day, so I'd fit them in some time—as well as doing weight training three times a week on Monday, Wednesday and Friday, from 6 am to 7 am, before getting ready for school. Each morning I'd get on the bus with the other year 11 and 12 students and head to the local high school, Lake Ginninderra College (LGC).

That first day walking into LGC, I was pretty apprehensive about starting at a new school, especially after my first years at Murray High, but I needn't have worried. We got off the athletes' bus, all wearing our AIS sweats and tracksuits, and made our way to class. All the other girls our age were beautifully dressed and wearing makeup, and we walked in as a group of athletes, and I remember thinking, 'This is who we are, this is who I am, I'm an athlete!'. Looking back on it, my whole identity had revolved around just that, right from the word go. I was an athlete, I never wanted to be anything else, I didn't know anything else. Because I was around other athletes who were also training all the time, no one looked at me as a gawky teenager. I'd always felt different, like I didn't fit in, but at the AIS I was accepted. All the men's basketball players were there, so I was finally going out with guys who were taller than me. I never had to pretend to be anything other than who I was. I felt like a teenager should feel in high school, which was awesome. No one was going to mess with me again, no one was going to tease me again, and they never did. That's a lesson for all teenage kids—you have to get through those few years of uncertainty, but always be yourself.

I'd been selected for the AIS, picked for the national junior team, my career was taking off, and I felt like I had a pretty privileged life after that. I got whatever I needed, all the resources were on hand, I didn't know any different,

I didn't *want* to know any different. Life just happened and it was happening fast.

I still had to go to school, that's simply one of those things. Years 11 and 12 at Ginninderra were set up as a college-type system, not nearly as rigid as I'd experienced in my junior high years. We'd have a class in the morning, come back to the AIS and have training or shooting, and then go back for afternoon classes if we had any. I would often be exhausted after the midday training and just want to watch *Dirty Dancing* or listen to Marilyn Manson or whatever I was doing back then, but above all, I wanted to sleep. When you're 15 and the only thing you do is train, all you want to do when you stop is sleep.

Sport was the priority at the AIS. They did try and get me to attend school, but I was persistently not an academic student, I really didn't care. There was only so much pushing they could do. They kept asking me to go to meetings and counselling but I didn't want to be studying, and they couldn't make me. Mum and Dad just wanted me to be happy. And I was. I was living, I was in my element at the AIS, because for me it was all about basketball and sport. I simply didn't enjoy the schoolwork.

We were playing in season a lot of the time, which meant plenty of training, and if we were in camps, we'd simply miss school. The AIS had a learning centre, so we did have work to do there, and every night we'd have two hours of homework in the study hall, and that was a drag for me. One night I was sitting there eating a pack of Pringles and my AIS coach Phil 'Brownie' Brown walked in. That was rare, it happened maybe once in the entire time I was there. He came in and took away my Pringles and got into me for eating in the study hall, and I thought to myself, 'This is dumb!'. I didn't understand the whole need for any sort of study until much later in life. Brownie was the AIS Women's Basketball Head Coach, including for our development squad made up of high school kids at the AIS playing against adult players in the Women's National Basketball League (WNBL)—for experience, mostly, we were never expected to win against fully grown women.

As well as being our coach, Brownie had to take on all these different roles, he was our boss, he mentored us, and became a bit of a father figure. There was a guy in the men's basketball program the first year I was there, he was a bit older than me and in his final year, and I really liked him. As soon as I met him I instantly wanted to stay around him, be near him—I guess he would have been my first real love interest. But then he went out with a few other female athletes, and I found out. I remember thinking, 'Well, that's not very nice!'. We weren't officially together, but I thought we were getting to that point. We're still friends and I found out years later that Brownie had taken him aside and told him to stay away from me, but I didn't know it back then, and the rejection had really hurt. Brownie was just being protective, that was the sort of role he took on, he looked out for us. With Brownie I was a kid, playing basketball with other teenage kids.

I'd felt isolated on the Australian junior team when I first started with them, but as my teammates from the AIS development squad grew into better basketball players, they were invited to play with the Gems as well. Suzy Batkovic was like a sister to me, she was already at the AIS when I started, and I'd already played with her in the NSW Country team from when we were about 12. Her mum was the first woman to buy me a sports bra, even before my mum did. It was green, I remember. I'd never seen a green sports bra before, and I remember telling Suzy that hers was amazing—she had boobs then, I didn't. Her mum went out and bought another the same and gave it to me. I was so chuffed, I'll never forget it.

When we were young, Suzy and I butted heads. She also has a super-strong personality, and you don't want to mess with her. When we were just kids, we didn't know how to deal with each other's personalities, but at the end of the day I'd go to war for that girl.

Kristen Veal joined the AIS from South Australia. We were the same age, and she also came on to the junior team, and is still one of my closest friends. Kristen was a point guard (number 1), Suzy is only an inch or two shorter than me and generally played centre (number 5) position. The centre tends to be the tallest in the team, whereas the point guards are usually the shortest. I was also playing centre, but became more of a forward–centre as time went on. The position I played became interchangeable between a 4 and a 5 as my skills developed. Unusually for the time, as a player

I was agile, could shoot the ball from outside the key and was also tall enough and strong enough to play inside, which is more of a power forward (4) player's role. In total, 11 former or current AIS girls were selected to play with the Gems that year, and having Suzy and Kristen, all those girls who were my age, join me in the Gems was pretty cool. We were friends and we ended up being queens of the court together. We turned out to be an extraordinary group of players who went on to achieve many individual accolades that I don't think will ever be matched in terms of world basketball.

We played in Europe, Japan, Brazil and Russia. The Brazil trip was for the FIBA Youth World Championship for junior players, and is held once every four years, the year after the Olympics and the year before the FIBA Women's World Championship for senior players aged 19 and over. Four years earlier, the Gems had taken out the youth championship for the first time, and the pressure was on for us to do the same.

We played seven games in eight days, losing the first game to Russia, but progressing with wins against the US, Spain, Cuba, Japan and Brazil to get into the finals, where we had to play the US for gold. It was a tough game, very physical. They were pounding us, pushing us off balance and trying to tire us, we'd react, and get into trouble for fouls (breaching the rules). You have to leave the court when you've been pulled up after five fouls, and the coach has 30 seconds to bring another player in off the bench. Usually a foul is given for doing something overtly physical against an opposition player, and the five top starter players on our team were all out by the time the game was drawn at 66 points each at the final buzzer. We went into overtime, where both teams play multiple five-minute periods until there is a winner. Tamika Catchings for the US scored a two-point basket and they were leading 68–66, and then we fouled and the US got a free throw. This is an unopposed shot at the basket from the free-throw line, which is generally given after a foul on the shooter by someone in the opposing team, and it's worth one point if it goes in. A three-point field goal, or three-pointers, are those shot from outside the three-point line, over 6 metres away from the basket. Two points are awarded for successful field goal shots taken inside that three-point line.

The US made the free throw, and on the second attempt at the free throw, we rebounded, managed to get the ball after the opposition missed a shot, and came back.

With one minute to go, the US was leading 76–72. We closed in to within two points with 30 seconds to go, the score 76–74. The US were awarded another free throw and they crept ahead to 77–74, and then with just three seconds left they successfully converted another free throw, and won 78–74. It was a tense game, and we could have won, should have won. We took silver.

I love the contact and the physicality of basketball, but by the end of a match against someone like the US, you're completely drained. After a big game, once the adrenaline has left your body you can't move, can't think, it's physically exhausting. We thought we would win and were pretty disappointed with the outcome, but all in all, after losing that game to Russia early in the round, we did well to get to the final and were relatively happy with the result. No one likes losing, but that's sport.

That night, all the teams gathered at the resort where we were staying in Natal and we had a big Brazilian beach party. It was a really fun atmosphere, with the camaraderie between teams and countries, and it was my first real taste of the social aspect of basketball, interacting and partying with other nationalities. I was a teenager embarking on life, with an incredibly talented group of young women from all over the world—it was the start of all our international careers. That was a fun crazy night, a night to remember.

6

...

Opals

Being part of the national team trumped everything, so as well as playing with the Gems I was still competing around those commitments with the AIS development squad in the WNBL. We were all juniors in the AIS team and not expected to perform as well as the stronger adults, but we made it to the finals that year and ended up coming fifth in the league, a very respectable result. I was awarded Rookie of the Year in the WNBL and was awarded the monthly AIS Sports Star that July, and just after returning from Brazil in August I received an invitation to attend the Australian seniors camp.

When I found out I felt completely overwhelmed. At 15, I was going to an Opals camp, something I'd dreamt about for so many years was actually happening, I would be playing for Australia. By September 1997, less than a month after playing overseas for the Gems, I flew out with the Opals to the US and then Brazil to play two invitational tournaments.

Joining the Opals was the most refreshing experience of my life. I was a little apprehensive at first, fearing it was going to be like playing with the Gems for the first time, but it was the complete opposite. The older girls on the team took me under their wing. Rachael Sporn, Sandy Brondello, Shelley Gorman, they all made that experience so much easier for me. Those three in particular, before the days of ready access to internet and email, would write me letters and just be really inclusive, making it a smoother transition for me. The captain, Robyn Maher, was 37 and had even played basketball with my mum. All these mature women treated me like their little sister, and that changed me, I wasn't so jaded going on trips with the Opals. I still had trouble with flying, but I didn't hate going away anymore.

The first trip was to Colorado in the US, and I vividly remember my first game, I was so nervous. I was subbed in for my first minutes as a national team player, an Australian Opal, and felt overwhelming pride and apprehension, but forgot where I was meant to be on the court. I went blank momentarily, but I went out there, got the ball at the top of the three-point line and took a shot. The ball went straight through the basket, not even touching the rim. It was so sweet, and it was at that moment I thought, 'Okay, I can do this, I can actually be here and do this!'.

Tom Maher was the Australian women's senior coach, and that man was the toughest coach I ever had. He got the best out of me—he also instilled a culture of toughness among the Opals players, and that's what I stepped into. He didn't sugar-coat anything, he just said what needed to be said. Tom was a hard-arse coach, he was tough. I remember thinking, 'If I do this right, if I shoot it straight, he's not going to yell at me'. When he shouted at people to shoot straight, everyone in the stadium would stop and look at whoever he was yelling at. I hated that, especially when I was younger, but he knew how to get the best out of all of his players. He also demanded perfection, which was impossible, but we all wanted to be perfect for him. I tried, but even though I got nowhere near it he still gave me a lot of direction and focus. At that time, I don't think anyone else could have got the best out of me like he did, maybe because I needed that toughness to really motivate me to want to be better. Personally, I thank him for that, and I think the Opals' success began with him. Tom made our group of basketballers one of the finest teams in the world, and his legacy was that the Opals became a global force for a long time.

With the Opals, I travelled everywhere. Travelling on planes was still really difficult, but by the time I was 16 years old I'd flown so many times, and I felt so happy being in the Opals with those older women, that I started to become a little better with it all. I was never comfortable flying, but at least I wasn't hyperventilating and crying all the time. We had that trip to Colorado in September, and Brazil at the end of 1997. Then Brazil again in early 1998, followed by Japan, Slovakia and Portugal in the lead-up to the 13th FIBA World Championship in Germany in May, just after my 17th birthday.

That two-week tournament is the biggest one for us outside of the Olympics. It was all still new to me, playing in the seniors, but once I stepped on to the court I wasn't afraid of making mistakes, I wasn't afraid of doing anything wrong. It was a really encouraging environment, the team wanted me to do well, they genuinely did, as friends and mentors. I was the baby of the team and any opportunity I got, I went out and took it. It was a great environment for my development, it was fun, and I just played. Anyone can get points on court, any player.

I guess when I was coming through, there weren't too many players with both my height and agility. I could shoot the ball from different places, and because I could shoot it was difficult for people to guard (defend) me—and I could also drive and play inside the key. Technically, I was playing three different positions on the court. At that time, there weren't too many people my size who could do that, so I was something of an anomaly. There were traditional post players who were my size, and they would play predominantly inside the key, they wouldn't be outside as much as I was. They didn't have my speed, or weren't able to move like me, and that was the difference. There are some special kids coming through now who are my height and can do all of those things and better.

In Germany, we made it through to the semi-finals without a loss, playing against Brazil, Cuba, Congo, Slovakia, Germany, Hungary and Spain. For the first time in a world championship the Opals had the chance of a gold or silver, but only if we beat the Russians in the semi.

Our shooting let us down, we only landed 30 per cent of our field-goal attempts and the Russians beat us 82–76. Despite the missed chances with our field goals the Russians had only beaten us by six points, and although there was disappointment in the locker room after the game, Tom told us to concentrate on the game for bronze against Brazil that was less than 24 hours away. The Brazilians were the defending 1994 champions and they wanted that bronze, but so did we.

We'd been playing against the Brazilians in the lead-up to the world championships and really knew each other's game. Our first game in the rounds against them had been tough, we'd only beaten them by one point. In the bronze medal match, we were in trouble at the start. Brazil were ahead in a 16–2 run in less than four minutes, and just before half-time they still led by 14 points. We fought back, but were still 12 points behind at half-time. In the second half, we came out and five minutes after the break wiped the deficit with a 15–3 run, before Annie La Fleur nailed a three-pointer ten minutes later. We took out bronze with a score of 72 to their 67 points. It was the first time the Australian senior team had won a medal in the FIBA World Championship, and everyone was over the moon, it was great. The US downed Russia 71–65, after our match.

Mum came to those championships, and it wasn't until she was there with me that I realised that she'd done it all before, she'd played at two world championships. She must have been really happy, as she has a photo of the two of us in the hotel in Düsseldorf in Germany that takes pride of place on top of her cabinet at home. I'm so glad I was able to share all of that with her. Whenever my parents were around I always performed better, especially when I was younger, I don't know why. A more supported feeling, perhaps. No matter what happens, I know Mum and Dad will be there, and that has always been my definition of safety and comfort. It didn't matter whether I performed well or terribly, I knew that they would always support me and always love me. I still feel so blessed because of them.

There were a lot of US scouts at the championships. The WNBA had just started, and they saw me there—so I guess, looking back now, that tournament was my coming out into the world.

7

...

The Stare

After the world championships, the media were everywhere. I had telephone interviews with different journalists, others came to our home with photographers, even a TV crew visited to do an interview. It was probably the first time I felt I was really in the national spotlight. I was still so young and there was a small part of me that felt like a bit of a fraud, I never believed I deserved any accolades. With all of the media hype, it felt good when I was able to get back out and play.

As well as being in the Opals and playing for the AIS, I was also still playing in the under-18s NSW Country squad, though the constant playing without a break was having an impact on my body. Coming into the NSW Country competition I had a sore shoulder and knee after the world championships, and sat out two early games. I was playing so much basketball that I started to appreciate the times when I could have a game or two off. I could still enjoy the game, supporting the team from the bench, and it was great to play in the same team with Chelsea, my best friend from Albury, again. We shared a room and talked about everything, anything, played music, I was obsessed with Marilyn Manson, INXS, Tina Turner and John Lennon at the time, and we played it all, loud. Spending time with her reminded me what it was like to be a kid again.

Music was and still is an important part of my life. Whether it's on in the background when I'm at home or providing motivation before games, it's always around me. People prepare for games differently—whether it be with music, or silence in your own head, visualising plays, it evolves over time for each person. Managing that in the locker room can sometimes be hard, some players want to listen to loud music, some want to listen to their music independently on headphones. I was that person, I had the earphones in. When I had my music on, I felt like I could control my surroundings and I was able to focus better.

I also had a game face that people would later talk about, 'The Stare', but it wasn't fire in my eyes as most people thought, it was just me getting ready for a game. Debbie Cook, my coach from NSW Country, taught us about imagery. She talked to us about imagining technical aspects of the game, a shot going in, a rebound, a good defensive play, always imagining playing at our best when we had down time before games, and I have done it ever since. If I was nervous or scared, that's the way I'd prepare myself in my head, to get ready for the play ahead.

On the court, if I had The Stare, the badass look, on my face it was me visualising what I was going to do next. If it was there before I went on to the court, I'd be seeing myself doing things before they happened, seeing what I was going to do in the game. When I was younger, I felt a bit like the world was against me, not for any specific reason, I just always felt like I was on an island of my own, and I acted tough as a type of protection. I think it was simply a coping mechanism. I knew how to get myself ready, prepare for what was ahead, I wasn't going to be intimidated by anyone, it was kind of like preparing for battle in a way. I was getting myself into a position to fight, ready to do anything. I knew it was going to be hard and that it would hurt, but you can't just walk on court without preparing yourself. That focus helped me play a physical, aggressive game.

Every game I would put myself into a state where I would see myself dominating my opponent, even if it was for just ten seconds. That's what The Stare was for me, I think. It was a way of refocusing thoughts in my head, talking myself into what was about to happen, feeling how I was going to play. We would warm up before each game, then come out and give the rest of the team a high-five, and stand and listen to the national anthem or wait for the other team to come out. I would use that time to see myself shooting a three, or rebounding, getting a steal, blocking a shot or just dominating in the game. To get into that state of mind was hard to start with, but as I got better at it, I didn't even realise I was doing it. If my head wasn't in it, I may as well not have been there.

Basketball can come naturally, but pushing yourself that bit further doesn't. You have to get yourself into a frame of mind where you'll do anything for those two hours. When you're in the throes of a basketball game you just react, it's instinct, you're playing with a team, you're relying on your training and how you get things done, you're being a basketball player. But if there was a break in play or a steal or a foul or whatever, I always took that time to try and refocus and gather my thoughts, catch my breath and get back into that focused state of mind, even though it was emotionally and mentally draining. Everybody has their own way of preparing for games, that's how you get to the top.

I had another ritual that started about the same time. Nike had become my sponsor and they looked after me for many years with shoes and clothing. I developed this ritual where I'd write on the tops of my Nikes—little messages to motivate me, or something about someone I didn't like, as a way to rev myself up further. As I got older those messages became more high energy, a reminder to myself to snap back, concentrate. Whatever motivated me or whatever it took to be reminded to focus, to get me there, I'd write it on the tops of my shoes. It worked because the more I had my hands on my knees catching my breath in games and in practice, the more I was looking at my shoes.

■ ■ ■

China came out to Australia to play in the Maher Cup in September 1998. The tournament was dedicated to our long-serving captain Robyn Maher, and would become an annual event. We played in stadiums around the country, from Dandenong in country Victoria, to Homebush, site of the upcoming Sydney Olympics. The Opals defeated China in all four games.

Next, the US came out to play the Goldmark Cup. We had five matches in the tournament and were without Michelle Griffiths, Trish Fallon and Carla Porter, who were all playing in Europe. I was yet to be a starter for the Opals, I was the reserve centre. Jenny Whittle, or 'Harley' as we called her, was set for a showdown with the US centre DeLisha Milton. As a team, we were about to play arguably the best in the world.

The first match was at the Derwent Entertainment Centre in Hobart. We were constantly pushed away from the post by their more muscular team, but defensively we were playing well, reducing their successful field goals to just 25 per cent of attempts in the second half. I'd come off the bench and managed a game high of 20 points, and blocked five shots (where you stop your opponents from scoring by blocking their shot with your hand, without fouling). Being the height I am, blocking shots was easier than for the shorter players, but you still have to watch the ball and pick your timing so as not to be fouled. With just 29.9 seconds left in the game, a free throw was awarded our way. Harley stepped up to take the free throw and popped it in, bringing our score to 68–63, the final score.

The second game was at the Glasshouse in Melbourne. The US led by four points with three minutes remaining in the first half, but we managed to reel off eight points by half-time and were leading by four. It was getting physical under the basket, and with ten minutes left in the game all four of the US centre players had been fouled out. We won, with a final score of 62–51.

We were two games up in a best of five tournaments as we headed to Adelaide. It was a tight game right up to the last quarter. With ten minutes remaining we opened up a lead of five points, the score 54–49, but a lot can happen in ten minutes on a basketball court. The Americans fought back, landing 11 points to our two in the next four minutes, followed by a three-pointer with five minutes remaining. I followed it with a trio of three-point plays, and the score was US 63 points, Australia 62, with four minutes remaining. The US hit back and with three minutes left the score was US 67, Australia 64. We managed to tie the score with a minute to go, before Kristi Harrower landed a three-pointer. Final score 70–67. We'd won the game, and the tournament, against the best team in the world. The US won the following two games in Wollongong and Sydney, but the cup was ours.

■ ■ ■

The AIS development squad had come in fourth in the 1997/1998 WNBL season, after being placed fifth in 1996/1997. We were put into the WNBL to improve our skills, and no team of teenagers was ever expected to do much better than bottom of the ladder. Halfway through the 1998/1999 season, Brownie pulled us all into the common room at the AIS and told us there was a very real chance that we could win. He asked, did we as a team want to continue playing the season as a development program, or did we want him to coach us for real, to win a championship? The answer was, unanimously, 'Coach us for real!'.

A development program meant that he had to try to give everyone a run, get everyone on the court, give us all an opportunity, and I think once we decided we were there to win in a professional women's league the stronger players tended to get more on-court time. I don't think my role changed though. I really only had one role, we all did, and that was to help our team win games. I know I'd made the national senior team, but no one person is more important on a team than the next. It was just basketball, competing was all I knew, and that's what I loved doing. Those girls were my peers, my friends, and we were having fun.

At the start of the WNBL season, we'd lost to Sydney and then won the next nine games in a row leading up to the final matches. We beat Jenny Whittle's team the Perth Breakers in the semi-final, 81–62, to take a berth in the grand final, with Harley's team having to back up and play Adelaide Lightning in the preliminary final. Perth beat Adelaide 67–46, and we were set to play them again. The stakes were high, the last time the AIS had even come close to a finals match was in 1983, but we did it! We beat Perth in the finals. The AIS development squad—a bunch of high school kids—had won the national championship of the entire WNBL. We were that good. For the AIS to win the national champion-ship was huge, and the achievement has never been repeated, before or after that season.

The core of the AIS team—me, Suzy, Kristen, Belinda Snell, Penny Taylor and Deanna Smith—went on to represent Australia for many years. Kristen took out the Grand Final Most Valuable Player (MVP), and I took out the WNBL MVP. With the highest field goal percentage, 54.1 per cent, and averaging 23.2 points per game, I was top scorer for the season. We were a team of kids simply trying to get better. I don't think we realised back then how big that win was, but in years to come we would. Something like that just doesn't happen, in any sport.

■   ■   ■

In my last two years of high school I was playing for NSW Country, the Gems, the AIS team in the WNBL and then the Opals. I was away from home, I was young and enjoying the ride, I was partying. I guess in those days we weren't as closely monitored as they are now at the AIS, we were able to sneak out a bit. In my final year of high school, I'd missed 90 something days of school. I couldn't manage it all, and study back then had never been my priority.

I sat the HSC at the end of 1998, but I failed, I don't know what mark I got, but I think it was in the 40s, out of 100. I remember sitting down for my HSC English exam and reading the essay question. I hadn't studied, hadn't been at school probably for three or four months, and I ended up writing about how much I loved Michael Jordan. I remember thinking that it was all a waste of time. I walked out of that exam and went straight to the courts for practice and never gave it another thought. I was playing basketball.

8

...

Tilley's

When my schooling finished, I was on the Olympic athlete program in preparation for the upcoming Sydney Olympics, and I'd also signed up with the Canberra Capitals WNBL team for the next season. I moved out of the AIS dorms and rented an apartment in Belconnen with fellow AIS player Deanna Smith. I remember the first time I had to pay my own bills, that was a bit of a shock, that and the feeling they always seemed due.

Around the corner from our apartment was the iconic Tilley's Devine Café Gallery. When I was still living at the AIS some of the team would go and see live shows there, but I didn't really find it until after I moved out. It was a great place to go for a coffee, a drink, a meal or to see live music.

We used to enjoy the odd glass of wine in those days, like most Aussie school leavers who reach drinking age. Tilley's would be open after games, after practice, had great food, and it just became our social hangout. Once I found that place I spent most of my down time there.

Tilley's became a sponsor of the Capitals, and it was where the whole team went after games. I'd been going there for about eight months before I met the owner, Paulie. I was really intrigued to know how Tilley's had come about, how she'd built it up. Paulie had started Tilley's in the early 1980s. A single mum with two kids, she decided to build a place that was safe for women. So at a time when Canberra had exclusive men's clubs, the only way a man could get into Tilley's was with a woman. Then men started complaining— which was strange, as women certainly weren't complaining about not getting into the exclusive men's clubs.

By the time I found the place, Paulie's kids were out of the nest and she worked there all the time. She's still a workaholic. She'd be there at six in the morning and still be there until the last shift finished. I spent so much time at Tilley's that Paulie and I became good friends, and we would talk and have these great conversations. She's such a fascinating person, because of what she's achieved, and what she believes, and I think that was the most important part of our friendship. We would enjoy a coffee or wine together and talk, and there was something that really drew me to those conversations.

Paulie made me aware of issues outside my cocoon of basketball, and that was what I needed in my life at that time, otherwise I think I would have become the most ignorant human being to walk this earth. I was quite uninformed about everything going on around me, whether it be political, social or economic, I didn't have the education behind me to understand it. I was an athlete, I didn't really think outside of being an athlete. Athletes spend so much time in their own head, thinking about themselves, and not about what is going on in the world around them, and I don't believe I was evolving into an aware, smart or good individual. Having Paulie enter my life at that time definitely opened my eyes, and I saw things I wouldn't ever have noticed before.

I was so young, so self-centred. I'd talk with Paulie a lot about myself, and I became fairly open about everything going on in my life. At one stage, I had an agent who'd call and order me around, and it got to the point where it really upset me, and the thought finally occurred to me, 'You can't talk to me like that just because I'm young!'. Paulie broke that behaviour down for me, talking about power and control so I could comprehend it all. She could identify things like that and I couldn't, she would explain and I'd think about it, how it would pertain to the feelings I was having. It was impressive, it taught me to identify an issue and then step back and critically figure out how I was going to deal with it, instead of shutting down and not thinking about it. Well, most of the time. She also helped me find a bit of power in myself that I didn't realise I had. The relationship between myself and that agent finally broke down, and

I actually walked away, which was a huge thing for me. She helped me to figure out how to work through relationships with people I couldn't walk away from, even though I'm still not terribly good at navigating those relationships where I feel I'm being pressured. Paulie helped me grow up, she was a large part of my development as a person.

She also gave me an appreciation and awareness of social issues, of the difference between men and women socially, of inequality between the sexes—back then it wasn't being highlighted or talked about as much as it is now. Paulie was so passionate in her beliefs about gender inequality that in the beginning I would think, 'Come on, what you're saying is too much'. It wasn't until I started to live it, that I came to understand it. I learnt a lot from her about feminism and gender inequality. I took in everything that she told me, and it blew me away.

I really gravitate towards strong personalities, and Paulie is certainly one of them. When relationships of mine have broken up, I've always gone to her to talk about it. She's an ear, a mentor and a good friend. We can say whatever we like to each other, our conversations are an open playing field—she tells me if I'm doing the wrong thing, and she's probably the only person, other than my parents, who can do that. Paulie was someone I could talk to throughout my career, and she's a great friend even to this day.

I bought my first house in the suburb of O'Connor on Paulie's advice and lived there when I was playing in Canberra. I bought it when house prices were quite low and set about renovating it. Looking back, the renovations were terrible, if you can image an 18 year old renovating. I put in blue carpet and painted the walls blue as well. I thought it was amazing, but it was truly horrible. Luckily it was in a good location, and location, as I learnt, was key in real estate. I sold it two years later, just after the property boom started, and made about $200 000. Paulie's advice was once again right on the mark.

There would be times ahead when I wished I'd remembered all she'd taught me.

9

. . .

Towards 2000

Playing for the Opals and in the WNBL, I had so much drive. I was 18, really tall and lean for my size, my body was still developing its strength, and the Sydney Olympics were 18 months away.

Cuba came out to Australia to play in the second Maher Cup, and the media were everywhere. The five games were to be in Melbourne, Bendigo in country Victoria, my home town of Albury for the third game, then Canberra, with the final to be held in Wollongong. We won the first match in Melbourne 80–58, and at the presentation ceremony it was announced that Robyn Maher was retiring, after playing her 374th international basketball game for Australia. Robyn was 39 years old, with two kids, and had decided to retire pre-injury, something every professional athlete hopes for.

With Robyn's retirement, Michele Timms became the captain. Timmsy had been the face of basketball in Australia when I was growing up. I looked up to her, she'd already been playing in the WNBL in the US for three years, and she was truly iconic in the world of Australian basketball. She had a global attitude and was a great player, and even at 33 she was amazing. Watching her try to keep her knees strong and free of injury was inspiring, there was a lot of work she had to do off the court to make it.

The Cubans were tough, it was a physical tournament. Physicality is inevitable in basketball, especially under the basket, where elbows are out and you have to use your body to take hits and give hits. Anything goes, as long as the referee doesn't see and call a foul on a player. We won the first two games, and the third game against Cuba was one of my career highlights, in front of a sell-out crowd packing the Albury Sports Stadium. I was home, playing for my country, in front of my mum and dad, Ross, Nanna Bennie, my aunties and uncles, some cousins and a lot of people I'd grown up with and cared about, and I felt so proud. With all of these people who were so special in my life watching, I scored the first nine points of the game. There are some moments you never forget and that was one of them. Timmsy hit a great three-pointer just before half-time, but Cuba didn't want to give up the tournament and fought back to within five points—they were tough. There were plenty of fouls but it was still a great game, which we eventually won 85–73. I'd managed a total of 30 points for the game and pulled down 11 rebounds, and felt on top of the world. The Opals went on to win the Maher Cup, taking all five matches.

Next, we took on Brazil—silver medallists at the 1996 Atlanta Olympics—in the Goldmark Cup, playing in Darwin, Adelaide, Melbourne, Hobart and Geelong. Timmsy, Kristi Harrower and Jenny Whittle were back playing the WNBA season in the US at that stage, but we still won that tournament as well, beating Brazil in all five games.

It was then our turn to travel overseas, this time to the US for two tournaments involving Poland, Brazil and the host nation. We went to San Diego first to play for the Olympic Cup, a tournament organised by the US Olympic Committee, which included basketball among several other Olympic sports. We beat the reigning European champions Poland and then Brazil in the first two games, only to be beaten by the US, but it was enough for us to play the US again in the finals. During that game the lead swapped a couple of times, but the US snatched the win from us in the last 20 seconds. In the second San Francisco tournament, we could only beat Brazil, losing to Poland on the buzzer, and then we were absolutely smashed by the US 94–68. We'd lost all of the lead-up games played against the US. After that, it was back to Australia and more training—the Olympics were under a year away.

Arriving back in Australia, I suddenly became the face of the WNBL. All the top basketball players had to go overseas to make a living from the sport, there was nowhere near the money to be earned playing basketball in Australia compared with playing in Europe, Asia and the US. The WNBL was trying to encourage more sponsorship to entice players to stay in the country. There were photo shoots, trips to Melbourne for the season launch, and then an event at Bondi Beach with players from other teams in new uniforms to promote the sport. There was certainly the interest in Australia, more kids were playing, more people were watching our games, but the sponsorship raised was never going to be enough to pay every player on each team a full-time wage.

The Capitals had been the wooden-spooners of the WNBL the previous year before I joined, and they'd signed up a new coach, Carrie 'Graffy' Graf. Graffy had a clean slate at the beginning of that 1999/2000 WNBL season. The Capitals may have sat at the bottom of the ladder, but Graffy had all the pieces in place for that year to be a success. As well as Shelley Gorman, a veteran player with the Opals who'd been in the team that won bronze at Atlanta, the Capitals had the three of us from the AIS team who'd won the previous WNBL championship—Kristen Veal, Deanna Smith and myself—as well as Karen Smith, El Sharp and Kim Wielens, who were already on the team and all good players in their own right.

Having a player like me on court who could do different things like shoot, block and rebound, and using Graffy's (then) non-traditional plays, which hadn't been seen before, we went from the bottom of the league to the top in one season, winning 16 of the 21 games played. In the major semi-final, we came up against the Adelaide Lightning, who were number two on the ladder. We went down 84–91, which meant we had to back up and win the preliminary final against the third-placed Bulleen Boomers in order to make the grand final. Although we managed to beat them 80–66, we'd lost home-court advantage, which meant we travelled to Adelaide to again play the Lightning, and won! For the first time, the Canberra Capitals took out the WNBL final. I finished the season as top scorer, with an average of 23.4 points per game, with Kristen topping the league in assists, and on my 18th birthday I was again awarded MVP for the 1999/2000 WNBL season.

We were all playing and training hard, motivated, the anticipation of competing in a home Olympics pushing us on. Every week I'd travel to Sydney from Canberra for training sessions from Sunday to Tuesday with Shelley Gorman and the Sydney girls. It was pretty full on. I had training with Graffy the rest of the week, so just the preparation itself was a full-time job. I think only Michele Timms and Michelle Brogan were playing in the US at that time, so we had the bulk of the Opals team still in Australia, and that was awesome, we could work together, build as a team.

Feeling privileged had become the norm. My career had taken off, I'd become an elite athlete, the Sydney Olympics were approaching, and I was treated well. I certainly wasn't the most approachable or appreciative person back then.

I didn't care when I was a kid. Kids do tend to be selfish until they have to take responsibility for more than just existing. It would certainly take me time to mature into respecting other people's positions, especially when everything was being handed to me.

Just before the Sydney Olympics, we played against the US at Rod Laver Arena in Melbourne to a sell-out crowd. Before every match, we'd go through and identify the strengths and weaknesses of the other team with the coach, and I'd look at the particular players I'd be opposing. Being a centre, in this match I knew I'd be up against Lisa Leslie, a player I'd always admired. I was completely in awe of her and her playing style. The first time I ever saw her was in the US, in an elevator, before playing against her at the end of 1999. She didn't say anything, and all I wanted was for her to say 'Hello', because she was a bit of a legend in my eyes. When she arrived in Australia it was clear that I was the up and comer, and she seemed so disrespectful towards me to the media, she'd be like, 'Lauren who?'. It was just this big game to her. I'm not one to be like that, I'm someone who will tell it how it is—to a fault that's how I am. She was clearly trying to make the point that I was irrelevant to her as a player, she wasn't intimidated by me at all, nor should she have been. But I couldn't help thinking that if she was making a point of writing me off, then she was actually really concerned, or at the least I was clearly on her mind.

There's a photo of me and Lisa Leslie from that Melbourne game, and it's me having a go at her and she's looking at me as if to say, 'What's your problem?'. We lost that match, but it wasn't the time to dwell on the negatives. We had an Olympic tournament to play.

The members of the Australian national women's basketball team announced for the 2000 Olympics were Sandy Brondello, Michelle Brogan, Carla Boyd, Jo Hill, Kristi Harrower, Shelley Sandie, Annie La Fleur, Trisha Fallon, Rachael Sporn, Timmsy, Jenny Whittle and myself. Kristen Veal had a chance of making the team as a point guard but had a motorbike accident in Sydney, breaking her hand, and that effectively put her out of the squad. My dream, the dream I'd told my mum about when I was a defiant 12 year old, was coming true—I was going to play in the Sydney Olympics for my country.

10

...

Sydney Olympics

I'd always felt a part of Sydney. I'm an Albury girl, but my dad's side of the family is from Sydney, and I'd spent much of my youth in Bankstown in the western suburbs with my Nan and Pop and auntie, uncle and cousins. The 2000 Olympics coming to Sydney was something very special for me, my family, and for all of Australia it seemed, the excitement and anticipation in the streets was palpable. For me, it was such a great atmosphere in which to be representing my country. I was meant to be there, I felt like I was destined to be a part of the Olympics. I'd thought about nothing else since the announcement all those years before, it had been driving me, motivating me. It's funny, but I think because the Olympics were in Australia, I felt I was in a safe space, there was no anxiety, no need to worry about having to travel.

That Olympic Games was a truly mind-boggling experience. Before the opening ceremony they ushered all the athletes together, ready for the national teams to march out at the end of the ceremony. We were sitting in one of the sport stadiums, The Dome, where we'd later play our basketball matches, with all the other countries, waiting for the parade of nations, and the Americans were doing their chant 'U-S-A! U-S-A!', in this massive stadium, drowning out all the others. I think it was Laurie Lawrence, the recently retired Australian swimming coach and liaison officer for the games, who stood up and got us all going, chanting, 'Aussie! Aussie! Aussie! Oi! Oi! Oi!'. We were shouting our chants so loudly back and forth. Laurie is hilarious, he's such a great motivator. That sort of in-your-face motivation has never really worked for me, but in an environment like that, it was incredible. He's probably the best person to have in the stands cheering on a team or trying to get others motivated, he's brilliant.

I went into those games not having experienced an Olympics before, and as a motivated, fit, 19 year old I just wanted to go out on the court and perform. I'd represented the national team for a couple of years and I felt like I was truly a part of the Opals, I'd finally become one of the 'go to' players for the team, and I was starting to take up the role of scorer. There was huge pressure, but I don't think I truly understood the enormity of the situation at the time. The chance of an Olympic gold medal didn't faze me too much, and it should have. I just went out and played.

Our first match was against Canada, and instead of being nervous the only thing I remember feeling anxious about was that I couldn't see my parents in the crowd. I started to worry that they weren't even there—but they were, and so were we, we won the game 78–46. We didn't have a match the next day, so I managed to catch up with family and friends after training, which was something I tried to do in breaks between games. Having Mum and Dad there was wonderful, I was sharing the whole experience with them.

Our next match was against Brazil, the toughest team to beat in our round of six nations, and with two minutes until half-time we were down five points. Carla Boyd turned a half-court steal into a basket, Sandy Brondello scored, Brazil answered and then Sandy went for another basket and slipped, kept control of the ball and put up a jump shot which found the basket as the half-time buzzer sounded. The crowd of 10 000 spectators in The Dome stood and cheered, and we were only halfway through the game. We crept forward over the next two quarters, it was a tough game. In the final quarter, Timmsy made a three-pointer from nearly halfway, with the last shot at the buzzer, and the crowd went wild, high-fives all around the team, the final score Australia 81, Brazil 70. Brazil was a tough team to match up against. Timmsy's basket probably made the margin a little more flattering than it should have been. The crowd at the game were awesome, so loud, the team felt in control and we were all playing so well. We were going for gold.

Two days later we beat Slovakia 70–47, and I was feeling pretty good and in control, I think the whole team did. Next, we played Senegal, and got out to a great start and blew them away early, but in the best tradition of African teams, Senegal were tough. Sandy copped a hit to the nose and it looked like it might have been broken, which was enough to get Timmsy slightly riled up, until Sandy calmed her down and pointed out that it wasn't intentional. We won 96–36, and again it felt like we were on a roll, we were fairly confident in our pool of players.

Two days later we played France. We'd played against them in the lead-up to the Olympics and they'd won twice in Europe against us. There was a real rivalry developing between our teams, especially when they were talking it up after those couple of wins. Kristi, who was my roommate at the Olympic Village, went to work on the court and made sure they were silenced in more ways than one. I was given a foul after becoming caught up with the French player Isabelle Fijalkowski trying to get a rebound—this was not uncommon, we'd developed a tough type of rivalry in the matches leading up to the Games. Isabelle thought I'd intentionally thrown an elbow at her, but I'd moved in order to get untangled and my arm swung around as she started falling off balance. Intentional or not I don't remember, but that was me when I was on the court, I never took a backwards step. Tom Maher took me straight off after the ref called the foul and told me to stay cool, to settle down and just concentrate. It was what I needed to hear, I felt the French didn't respect us. Sure they'd beaten us twice before, but we did win when it mattered, beating them at the Olympics 69–62. At that point we'd beaten all the teams in our group, and we progressed to the quarterfinals against reigning European champions Poland.

I was used to literally looking down on plenty of opponents, and for the first time I understood what it must have been like for them looking up at me. The Polish centre, Margo Dydek, standing at 2.18 metres (7 feet 2 inches), was the tallest female professional basketball player in the world. From the first jump ball, I remember looking up at her and wondering how I was ever going to go higher than her and win the tip. I would play against and with Margo for many years, and she became someone I was very fond of. She married an Australian years later and I met up with her and her husband David and her two little boys in Queensland at an event I attended in 2010, when she was coaching for Basketball Queensland. I was really looking forward to continuing our friendship, the professional basketball community is so small in Australia and we'd shared so many games, but was horrified—as was the entire basketball community—when she suddenly collapsed at home in 2011 and died while pregnant with her third child, who also died. It was shocking.

Back in 2000, Margo and I had such a competitive match up against each other, she must have thought I was the most annoying young player. Margo had led the 2000 Olympics in scoring and rebounding, but I gained confidence as soon as I scored over her, over someone that tall and someone that good. We won the match against Poland 76–48, and were to again face the 1996 Olympic silver medallists Brazil in the semi-finals.

I was nervous before that semi, we were so close to the gold medal game and I was anxious I'd blow the whole thing somehow. I shouldn't have been, Sandy scored six points straight out and we led 11–0 before Brazil fought back. Brazil were a great team of girls and my feeling was that if they did win, then I hoped they would win gold. We eventually beat them 64–52, and everything felt good in the team. We were playing for gold, against the best team, from the best league in the world—the US.

The US is a powerhouse, number one in the world, and in 2000 everyone else was just trying to get to that point. The American team had player after player to draw on, they could have put three teams into that Olympics and won gold, silver and bronze—they were that good, that strong. A couple of our players could probably match up with some of their players, but then again, we're notorious for punching above our weight.

We knew that our captain, Timmsy, was retiring after the Olympics, and we wanted nothing better than for her to retire with an Olympic gold medal around her neck. We were in a team meeting before the game against the US, and the Opals had never reached a gold medal match in any Olympics before, and one of the girls in our team said, 'No matter what, we'll get silver, we can't lose silver'. And I remember being taken aback by that remark and thinking, 'That's not good enough!'. Before that was said, all we had in our minds was the gold medal, and I didn't see the need for her comment. I guess for me it was just about winning the gold. Everything else I'd set my mind to I'd managed to achieve, winning gold was achievable as well, we'd got this far—anything can happen in a game.

I was again matched against Lisa Leslie. I like the physical aspect of the game, as much as it hurts, but out of all the teams we played, the Americans played so physically. In all honesty, I found myself in awe most of the time as I watched them warm up, and then again watching them play when I was on the bench. They were tough—it wasn't only to do with sticking elbows out or punching, it was just the way they carried themselves, their aura and confidence as a team. As their opponents, we gave back as good as we got. Basketball is about leaving nothing on the floor, standing with your teammates in the face of adversity and overcoming it.

That gold medal match was a tough game, the battle between Lisa and me became prevalent, and we were losing. In the second half, Lisa and I both went up for a rebound, I was behind her and my finger got caught in her hairpiece. I didn't know she had a hairpiece on, how would I have known? I certainly found out. My finger got caught in her ponytail as we went up for the ball and her hairpiece dropped on to the floor. In all honesty, it gave me a fright.

I thought 'What the?', and actually stopped and looked at it, before taking a step away from it. As I backed off I remember still thinking, 'What the hell is that?'. I looked at Lisa and thought I must have hurt her, I believed I'd actually pulled her hair out, but she snatched up the hairpiece and turfed it into the crowd—where I think it landed on a press photographer's face or lap. He grabbed it and held it up and waved it about, sending the crowd into hysterics, and they in turn all started calling out, laughing and pointing at Lisa, who was now sporting a very short ponytail. I remember running back down the court and having the American players shouting abuse at me, it was horrible, I was like, 'Oh god, what have I done?'. On the other hand, all the Australian girls were laughing. This was the gold medal match at the Olympics, we were 20 points down and we should have been crying about it, but everybody in our team was just in hysterics. It was a funny incident I guess. But it was an Olympic match, an important moment, and it was a very public arena for it all to play out in. Nobody wants to go through something like that, and I felt bad. I hadn't meant for anything like that to happen, there was no intention there at all. Life is so bizarre sometimes, it was so weird that something like that should have occurred between Lisa and me.

In everybody's eyes after that, we were rivals who had a healthy disdain for one another. But like I said before, I didn't dislike her, right from the beginning I was a fan. We'd played against each other previously, but she didn't know me, she didn't know who I was. Probably to a degree I tried to model my inside game on hers. She was also very tall, could score and was athletic, and that was what I wanted to be, I wanted to be as dominant as she was inside the key. I had some outside game as well, so that made us a bit different, but Lisa was very commanding inside the key. She was very crafty, and had some good moves, but that incident at the Olympics became the precursor for the rest of our careers.

We lost, 76–54. My dream, our dream, of winning gold was shattered, and it hurt. I'd felt so sure we were going to take the gold medal, especially after winning every game leading up to it. That assuredness had grown stronger, but we didn't play well in that final match, that's all there was to it. We won silver, which was the best performance of any Australian basketball team at an Olympics to that point, but it wasn't what I'd dreamt of since being a little girl, what had motivated me. The Americans had been the team to beat, they'd always been the challenge, and they'd won.

After the game, all the media wanted to talk about was Lisa Leslie's hairpiece, and Timmsy, as our captain, told them she thought it looked like a dead rat. Timmsy is hilarious, she will say whatever is on her mind, but then that's all of us to a degree. She really supported me through it, she had my back, all those women did, which is indicative of my whole Opals experience with that group, they were just amazing people. But still, the fact that people still come up to me and ask about that one incident all those years ago is pretty amazing, it's just a shame that such a memorable event was at someone else's expense.

Lisa was so dirty after that game. She spoke with the media, saying that she'd told me I could have the hairpiece as a souvenir, she'd take the gold. Oddly enough, I don't recall her actually saying that—I'm pretty sure I would have remembered her telling me something like that post-match. But she's right, she did get that bloody gold medal.

After the Olympics, I really needed to have a break, we all did. Paulie let us use her house on the South Coast, and a group of us travelled down after the Olympics. It was a beautiful place, paradise, in an isolated spot where we weren't going to be bothered by the media. There were about four or five of us I think, including our newly retired Opals captain Timmsy. I have huge respect for her and for all she's done for Australian basketball. She was one of the players back then who'd forged that path for us, there weren't too many players before my group who'd played overseas in the off season. She was one of the first Aussie WNBA players. There were pioneers of course, like my mum, who played over in the US in college, but they didn't have a professional women's league back then. Players like Timmsy, Sandy Brondello and Shelley Gorman were the first to play year-round, playing WNBL here in our summer then travelling over to the WNBA or Europe, doing a 12-month professional basketball circuit. I was about to find out how hard that life could be.

11

...

The Draft

Women's basketball in Australia was in the spotlight after the Sydney Olympics, and the Australian team had jumped into third ranking in the world behind the US and Russia. I think I'd played well individually, with an average of 15.9 points and 8.4 rebounds per game, funnily enough my best game being the final against the US, with a match high of 20 points and 12 rebounds.

My agent had been approached by the WNBA in the US and I was asked to their draft. The draft is held annually, with all the WNBA teams able to pick players from a pool of up-and-coming talent, mostly American college graduates— but occasionally international players are also invited. Most college players are about 21 or 22 years old by the time they've finished their studies, and to be asked to the draft is a rite of passage for any young basketballer, an honour every college player aims for. The US was where the serious play happened. In the WNBA draft, there is a strict payment structure, underpinned by collective bargaining between the players and the WNBA, giving teams who don't have as many strong, highly paid players a chance to get the better draft choices.

I was in a haze. I didn't know that much about it, and my agent had also been talking with an Italian team who wanted me to play with them in the Euro-League. The Italian offer was worth about AU\$600 000 a season, whereas first pick of the US draft earned about US\$52 000, but the WNBA was the place to play and the direction I was steered towards.

I'd had a break after the Olympics and over Christmas, and was enjoying being back playing with the Capitals. We came second in the WNBL finals, behind the Sydney Flames, in the 2000/2001 season, and I would have been perfectly happy staying in Canberra. I felt comfortable there, I was in the WNBL and the Opals, I had my own little world and I was fine with that. I had my own safe space, there was no anxiety. Being drafted would mean moving to the US and playing in the world's best basketball competition professionally. I'd been to the US a few times already, touring with both the junior and senior teams, but if I was picked, that would mean living there for months on end. A strange country, new people, and doing it on my own—I would be out of my comfort zone, well and truly. Deep down I didn't want to do it, but felt that I had to, because that's just what you did. If I wanted to be a professional basketballer, I had to be in the WNBA, and now was my chance.

In April, suppressing my trepidation, I boarded a plane with Mum and travelled to New Jersey for the 2001 draft. My agent at the time had met with the WNBA, and they'd suggested I might get into the top three, the three players most wanted by the teams, which was daunting, and created an additional fear—would I really be good enough? Mum hadn't been on a plane with me since I was 12, when my grandfather passed away and we had to fly to Sydney to meet Dad, and I was so glad she was there. To make my anxiety about flying worse, the flight over was horrendous, lots of turbulence, which was never good for me. I was so nervous about going to the draft, and scared. Where would I end up? I truly was in two minds, it was exciting to be asked, but there was such a large part of me that didn't want to be there.

My sponsor Nike picked Mum and me up in a limousine from the John F. Kennedy International Airport in New York and took us to the Empire State Building for a bit of sightseeing. We even went into a McDonald's drive-through in that great big limo. Nike were unbelievable, talk about glitz and the glamour, I went from being this country kid who played basketball in Australia to being driven around New York in a stretch limo, getting whatever I wanted for 24 hours. Mum and I finally arrived at our hotel room, completely jetlagged, and all we wanted was a coffee, but

I didn't know how to use the percolator (still don't). Instant coffee became my friend from then on, because it's the same in all countries, although it still tastes better in Australia.

That night before the draft I just started crying, I was so upset and scared. Mum stayed up with me all night, we played cards, watched movies, and as a result we were both zombies by the time we were driven to the draft on the WNBA bus the next day. We arrived at the venue and they put makeup on me and tried to pretty me up for the cameras, as pretty as one can be feeling jetlagged and nervous. If I went number one it was a big deal, I'd be called first, out of all the girls—college graduates, foreigners, everybody—and it would be televised on national TV.

We were sitting at a table and they called my name first, and then announced Seattle Storm had drafted me. I was so overcome I turned and kissed Mum, burying my head into her shoulder, not wanting to leave her side, before going up on to the dais. They handed me my number one jersey, which I held up for the press to photograph. All I can really remember is feeling completely overwhelmed. I was honoured to be number one, but I was so unsure about my future and the path I was about to undertake. I had no idea where Seattle even was, I thought it was on the other side of the country. I knew nothing about it, other than seeing the Tom Hanks movie *Sleepless in Seattle*, and now I was going to live and work there.

Mum and I flew to Seattle briefly to meet the coach and team, before our flight back to Australia. When we arrived in Seattle we were picked up by yet another limousine, which had Savage Garden playing in the back, and I remember thinking 'They clearly have no clue what music I am into'. We met Karen Bryant, CEO of the Storm, and my new coach, Lin Dunn, an eccentric and brilliant woman who I still have a lot of respect for. They took us to a major league baseball game, the Seattle Mariners were playing the Anaheim Angels. We had box seats, and as they flashed my face up on the big screen I was introduced to the 40 000 fans at the game as the city's new star basketballer. As if I wasn't nervous enough already. I was on the front page of their newspapers, on the TV news, greeted and welcomed at restaurants or when we went shopping, it was incredible, I kept thinking, 'How am I going to do this, by myself?'. Anything big that comes into my life, my initial reaction is that I can't do it, it's too much for me, the worst-case scenario always pops into my head, and that's what it was like going into the WNBA.

As I headed back to Australia to pack up my life, all I remember thinking was 'Can I really do this?'. I didn't have a choice, I had a responsibility to my new team.

12

...

Seattle

I said goodbye to everyone in Albury and Canberra and flew back to Seattle and moved into a beautiful serviced apartment above a convenience store near the wharves, which had been organised by the Storm. I think Seattle is the most stunning city in the world—well, the most stunning city outside of Australia. Seattle to me is like a mixture of Melbourne and Sydney. It's got the weather of Melbourne but it has the water of Sydney, no opera house or bridge, with beautiful water-ways. There's lots of greenery, the emerald city they call it, it's truly lovely. If I'd gone to any other city in that country, if I'd been drafted somewhere else, where I might have been miserable, where I maybe wouldn't have wanted to leave my apartment, then I probably wouldn't have played for long.

The US was larger than life, everything was larger than life, the stadiums, the cars, meal sizes, everything. The food was amazing, chicken wings and buffalo sauce or hot sauce—don't know what was in it, but I loved it and ate it all the time—lots of carbs. Everything you can eat here in Australia, you can eat there, just more of it. Because we were training and playing all the time, it usually didn't matter what we ate, but if I wasn't playing a lot of minutes, or if I was injured and was out for a week or two, I had to be really mindful of my eating, otherwise I'd just balloon. I felt like I did put on weight, but when I look back at photos now, I wasn't actually that big. When you're young you don't realise how lovely you really are, not until you're at an age when you no longer look as good.

The Seattle Storm colours are funnily enough green and gold, with a touch of a deep red. Our uniforms were predominantly white when we played at home, but green when we were on the road. One of the first things Seattle discussed with me was what number I wanted on my jersey. Numbers can have a lot of sentimental value to players, especially if, like me, your parents had played and had worn a certain number. I asked for and was issued with the number 15, Mum's old number. My mum, I don't think she realises how important she is to me, but she's been there through thick and thin. Not making waves, just being there to put an arm around me or give me a hug, and sometimes that's all I need. She's a good woman, and she was a great basketballer. With the Opals, number 15 was already taken, and if I wanted it

I would have to wait my turn. In Seattle, I think there was someone already wearing it, but because I was first draft pick and they were trying to make it special for me, they gave me number 15. That *was* special. In a funny way, it felt like Mum was with me, like I would be okay.

Going into training for the first time was so different from anything I'd experienced before, everything about being in the WNBA compared with playing in WNBL was just out of this world. The housing, cars, accommodation, where we played, where we trained, it was all incredible. We were affiliated with the Seattle SuperSonics, the men's team in the National Basketball Association (NBA), so our training facility was this massive gym and two courts decked out in SuperSonics and Seattle Storm signage. Everything about it, including the locker room, was larger than life and bigger than anything I'd ever seen or had to deal with before. Even playing at the Olympics didn't compare with how I felt playing in the US. I found the depth of the situation, the realisation that this was going to be my life, truly daunting. The entire organisation was so professional, I was in the big time, thrust into the spotlight—the media were at every practice session. If I walk into a situation I'm tentative about, I shut down, I become introverted, and it takes a little while for me to get normalised. So, when I walked into the gym for the first time I was meek Lauren, I felt so insignificant. It was just my way of coping, especially back then.

For a month before the season started we had training camp, and it was good to meet up with fellow Aussie Katrina

Hibbert, who I'd met briefly with the rest of the team after being drafted. Seattle had brought her into the league from the previous year's draft, their first year in the WNBA, from Louisiana State, which is also where my mum had played in the 1970s. I think Katrina scored the first two points ever for Seattle Storm, her claim to fame. We became instant friends, and this developed into a lifelong friendship—even though if we're together longer than 48 hours we can't stand each other! But she really is like a sister, and to this day she's the first person I call when I need a friend to chat to.

At the beginning of the camp there would have been about 20 of us. On the very first day, at the start of practice, after we'd warmed up, our coach Lin gave us this drill where she made us play five on five, but with no boundaries, no fouls being called, we just went hell for leather. It was so physical, but that's what typified the competitiveness of those camps, everyone fighting for a position on the team. I don't know why Lin did it, why she had that drill, but I think it was to see how much we all had in us, how badly we wanted to be there. Most of the other girls had come to the team after playing college basketball with hopes and dreams of becoming professional, but only a small percentage of basketballers get picked out of college for the draft. That's how it is, it's dog eat dog, nobody cares who they tread on to get to the top. It's the same with the men's league, you go out there, it's basketball, it's business. Here in Australia it's not, you're careful whose feelings you hurt, so it was really different over there, but that's what made the US very real for me. I felt like I had something to prove to try and make the team—but because I was the first draft pick, and pretty much guaranteed a spot on the team no matter what, I felt targeted by the other players. I'm not sure if that's what they thought, but I certainly did feel targeted.

Katrina and I became good friends during the camp, but when they picked the team she was cut and replaced by someone else, and she went back home. I was really sad seeing her go and it felt like my last link with Australia was gone. I would have to do this alone after all.

13

...

On with the Show

In the US, basketball games are a show, they really know how to put it on for the fans—there's music, lights and entertainment. The Seattle Storm was named after the city's propensity for winter storms and rain, though when I was there and playing in their summer I never saw that sort of weather. Their theme song for home games was AC/DC's 'Thunderstruck', which was perfect for an Aussie like me. They really played up that fact. Every time I landed a shot in a home game there'd be the sound of a didgeridoo playing, and when I was warming up they'd always put on an Australian song for me.

The Storm also had something called a Jumbotron, a great big electronic four-sided screen on top of the scoreboard—it was located in the middle of the court, up high, and they would show videos that players would make for the fans, interviews where they would get to know a bit about us and our personalities. There were also mini-games, and an all-kid dance squad who'd lead the young fans in a conga line on court to a pop song, it was all a lot of fun. It was glamorous, playing in these big arenas with huge numbers of fans, the atmosphere could be overwhelming at times, but it was awesome.

The 16 WNBA teams are broken up into two 'conferences'—Western and Eastern—and the finals are played between the best teams from each conference. The previous year, Seattle had come last in the WNBA Western Conference. The WNBA was still new to Seattle, and as well as the fact that I was the number one pick of that year's draft I was what they term a 'franchise player', something that was really pushed by the media. A franchise player is seen not only as the best player on the team, but also as someone who the team can build their franchise around for the foreseeable future. Being so young, and not having experienced anything like it before, I didn't understand what this truly meant, but I quickly found out.

It was made abundantly clear that my one role was to help the team win, to score points. I didn't initially understand this from the business perspective. I'd always been a good basketball player in my teams, but I didn't understand the concept of one player having all of the spotlight. My first professional game was against Phoenix Mercury in front of a home crowd.

The group of media at the game were pretty much the people who came to training, you'd usually have the same reporters covering every game. Their questions were always very blunt and pointed, I felt an enormous weight of expectation. I needed to make a very big adjustment to operate in a highly professional world of basketball that I'd never encountered before. Even though I had a degree of media exposure in Australia, I'd been protected a bit, especially at the Olympics, probably because of my age, the enormity of the situation and to keep me focused. Media appearances had been shared amongst the entire team. My media involvement had been pretty low key, and I just assumed that was how it was done. Suddenly in Seattle everyone wanted to know about me, talk to me. I think I blundered my way through it, but the pressure was intense. The team had put all their faith in me as a basketballer who would take the team somewhere other than last place.

We played 32 games over 11 weeks—it's a very compact season over there, you'd play three, sometimes four, games a week over a four-month season. You don't get a night off in the US. There are no easy games, so you can't take it easy, and I was training all the time. Basketball is a more physical game than a lot of other female sports, apart from perhaps women's AFL, but it really is a different type of physicality, you can't compare sports. I had a real chip on my shoulder when I first went over to the US, I knew people were saying I was an upstart, the young Australian coming into their league, and my only response to that was to arc up. I felt like my back was against the wall, and I fought. That year I had a record number of technical fouls given to me, but I had to play that hard to show people not to mess with me, because otherwise I would never have survived. People went after me physically, but I could handle it.

The Los Angeles (LA) Sparks, Lisa Leslie's team, were also in the Western Conference, so we'd come up against each other four times a season. With the hairpiece mishap still in everyone's mind, I knew it was going to be tough. It was unfortunate what happened in the Sydney Olympics final, unfortunate that it happened at all, and for the rest of my life people are going to associate me with that incident. Our battles, yes, they were absolutely battles on the court, she was without doubt one of the best players in history. But she wasn't the toughest opponent I ever had to face.

The LA Sparks were tough back in their day, they were probably the benchmark for all the other teams. Lisa and DeLisha Milton, who also played for the Sparks, could be quite rough, overtly physical, elbows flying, it was over the top, especially with me. I didn't deal well with it when I was younger, because I wasn't as physically strong as them, and I know I was a bit of a loose cannon. Sport is entertainment, but for the athletes it's everything, that's why we're there. It's serious for us, we don't know anything else, that's all we've done our whole lives.

I was very lean at that point, and I still played more of an outside game, so that I could shoot the ball from outside the key. Post moves—which involve putting your back to the basket, getting inside and pushing people around—still weren't my forte, I wasn't strong enough for that yet. We had a big Czech Republic girl at Seattle, Kamila Vodichkova, who'd represented Czechoslovakia in the 1992 Olympic Games, she was really strong and had a body on her, and she played 5 (centre) while I played the 4 (power forward) spot. Generally, the taller, larger players play in the 4 or 5 positions as we're better at post moves. To 'post up' you establish a position near the basket, especially if you have a smaller defender, and you face away from the basket to receive the ball so that your body can protect the ball from the defending player. This is where most of the overtly physical contact takes place. Lisa could push me around a bit, absolutely, because she was stronger and she was a better inside player than I was at the time.

The stadiums were always packed when Seattle played LA, there was always a lot of hype around it, the TV viewing audience was larger, people loved it. That incident at the Sydney Olympics had drawn so much media attention—a bit of controversy will always get you viewers, as I found out. Those LA Sparks and Seattle Storm games were often sell-outs.

We didn't win a single one of the three games we played against LA that season, but I played my hardest, and it showed in my stats, with some of my highest point scores achieved in those games. DeLisha Milton was the 4 player for LA, so we'd also match up against each other, and DeLisha was known for being physical. I ended up becoming a physical player as well, because there's no other way to combat a dominant power forward, it's hard when you can't score. Unless you put on weight, get strong and work that aspect of your game, you're just going to get pushed out. DeLisha is a lovely girl. It's so funny, the contrast between her personality when she is and isn't playing—off the court she's a beautiful human being, but on the court in opposition, you have to watch out. I would finish games covered in bruises, but I loved it, it made me feel alive.

My status as the number one pick, the fact I wasn't American, the hairpiece incident, none of those things helped my on-court battles. All of this made me feel low at times, and I was dreadfully homesick. Mum and Dad were still working and couldn't come over, and I was calling them every night. My phone bill was astronomical.

I missed home, but I was one of 11 Aussies playing in the WNBA that year. Two of my AIS team had also been drafted in 2001 alongside me—Kristen (13th in the draft) and Penny Taylor (11th)—and Tom was coaching in Washington. Halfway through the season we played Timmsy's team, the Phoenix Mercury, in Phoenix. Even though she'd retired from the Opals, Timmsy was still playing in the WNBA. Another Opals player, Trish Fallon, was also playing for Phoenix, and Graffy was the assistant coach. We won that game against Phoenix with the highest winning margin in the Storm's two-year history, and that night after the game we all went out, Timmsy, Trish, Graffy and myself. We talked, staying up until four in the morning, it was the best night. I hadn't had much time for socialising before then, it had been training, training and more training.

We only won 10 of the 32 games that year, and Seattle again came in at the bottom of the Western Conference ladder. Despite that, the people of Seattle were great, the fans, the team, the city, they were behind me and I felt, I knew, I could do better. I was chosen as an All Star that season, one of the top ten players from the Western Conference. An All-Star game, which takes place once each season, features the best ten players in each conference, and we would play against the Eastern Conference in an All-Star weekend match.

I was nervous before that first All-Star match. Playing alongside some of the best in the league in a showcase match was frightening to say the least, but what an honour. Lisa Leslie was in the team, along with Sheryl Swoopes, Tina Thompson, Ticha Penicheiro and Yolanda Griffith, it really was an eye-opener, and my confidence grew by being there. Given what had happened at the Sydney Olympics just the year before, I wasn't looking forward to the reception I'd receive, but my fears were mostly unfounded. I walked into the locker room and the 2000 US Olympic player Katie Smith walked up to me with a flower and said, 'A rose for my Aussie friend'. I felt relieved, most of the team were really nice and friendly when we played.

I'd been afraid of going to the US, and still by the end of the season I was in two minds about returning, because I'd been so homesick. For a while, I thought that maybe I wouldn't go back—but I did, it was just what I had to do.

Even though I didn't want to, in my head I felt like I had to, I had a responsibility to Seattle, and to myself.

■ ■ ■

After 28 games of basketball in the US, which were very physically demanding—much more so than any consistent runs of games I'd played before—my shoulder had broken down. It had started playing up when I was at the AIS and playing in NSW Country, and like a lot of my injuries, initially it wasn't diagnosed. I'd had numerous scans and they hadn't revealed anything serious enough to warrant surgery, so I played through the pain. I had full medicals before I started playing with most teams I joined, each having their own set of medical investigations, their own medical treatments.

It got to the stage in the US where I'd try and lift a can of Coke off the bench and it would hurt so much, the pain in my right shoulder was just so sharp, that it would physically stop me moving my arm. I knew the importance of getting up a certain amount of shots a day, I needed to do that for my own confidence, but that was still more time on court, pounding, jumping, and my body would react. The more I did that, the more my shoulder, my body, hurt. Before playing and practice I'd be taking five Ibuprofen tablets, an over the counter medication, because I found they helped with my pain. Every day for years this was my routine, even for shoot and run games, and for practice. I don't know how my liver still functions.

Arriving back in Australia, I had to have surgery on my shoulder. It ended up being diagnosed as a rotator cuff injury. I've still got the pins in my shoulder, they were meant to come out one or two years later but I've never had a problem, so I just left them, I haven't touched them. My shoulder had been a critical injury, if I hadn't had that fixed properly I wouldn't have played again. It's one of those injuries you can't really play through, so I took time off, and didn't take part in the start of the Capitals' WNBL season, returning mid-season instead.

We won the WNBL series for a third time, and this was the start of me playing on either side of the world each year. The Australian WNBL training camps would take place in September, then I'd play in the WNBL from October to February, finishing closer to March, so almost six months. Then I would normally train in a camp or two with the national team, before I went back to the WNBA in early May and played all the way through to August, and into September if we made the playoffs and finals.

I also still played for the Opals in between my WNBA and WNBL commitments. In May 2002 we travelled to Japan, where we won a tournament, before I returned to Seattle for the 2002 season. I was playing year-round, basketball was my full-time job.

14

...

Fly Like a Bird

I still had issues with planes. I didn't enjoy having to fly all the time, so I went to a psychologist to try and put some coping mechanisms in place, but they didn't work and I was prescribed Valium to calm me down on flights. And then something happened that exacerbated my fear and took it to a whole new level.

I was back home in Australia after the WNBA season, having a drink with friends one night at Tilley's after a music gig, and I happened to look up at the TV screen and thought, 'That's weird, must be a movie'. As I was watching a reporter talking, the footage of a passenger plane slamming into one of the World Trade Center buildings in New York was shown again. It was real! We were all suddenly glued to the broadcast. Then when the second tower was hit not long after, I was totally shocked, we all were. We kept watching as one of the towers collapsed less than an hour later, and then the other, with reports of another hijacked plane crashing. It was mindboggling. I had a friend in New York at the time, Sonja Henning, a fellow Storm player, and immediately texted her to make sure she was alright, but couldn't get hold of her.

The television coverage was constant, on every channel, and we were completely consumed by it. I managed to get in touch with Sonja in the days following and she told me she was safe, but like so many others we were young and had never in our lifetime been exposed to anything like it before. I wasn't very mature, and the attack instilled a further wave of fear in me, knowing I'd be travelling on planes all the time with my job, especially in the US.

For three or four days after that, I couldn't get out of bed, I just lay there watching it all unfold on the TV. The media coverage was running 24/7 and I was just completely stunned, and scared. The whole thought of getting back on a plane, any plane, was completely terrifying to me. I didn't know how to deal with it, I had few or no coping strategies, and my fear of flying had just compounded and grown exponentially.

The WNBL season started in October. September 11 had been so horrible, and it changed me, fed my anxiety. Being so young and quite sheltered, like every other kid in Australia at the time, it was the dawn of a new era for all of us, it was really frightening. I didn't want to go back to the US because I was afraid. But then I also remember thinking, 'There are so many brave people in the world who have to face things like this, who are facing it, pull yourself together!'. I told myself that I had to get on with it, but I was still an absolute mess before travelling back. In the end I just forced myself to do it.

When I returned to the US, airport security was over the top and didn't get any better after that. Security at American airports had always been tight, I remember thinking it was different from Australia, much tougher, even before September 11. I arrived back in Seattle shaken but wanting to train and play, do my job—and then a few days before the 2002 season actually started, I rolled my ankle badly in training. I'd rolled my ankle numerous times, 'No biggy' I thought, but by the next day my ankle and leg had turned black. I missed the first week of games, but rushed back to play thinking it was just a bad sprain, I'd had plenty of sprains before. I did get through the season on it, but after that season I started to experience really intense peroneal pain (pain in the area running alongside my fibula), but still kept playing through it, something I'd tended to do since I was 12 years old.

That second season with Seattle was where I first met Sue Bird. Sue is such an incredible person and an impressive player. A year older than me, Sue had been named New York State Player of the Year in high school and was invited to play in the All-American WBCA game for the top 20 high school students in the country. She then had four years playing at college, taking out Women's Basketball College Player of the Year in her final year, before making the number one draft pick in 2002. Seattle picked her up for the 2002 WNBA season, and in my opinion there has been no better point guard in the world previously or since. A point guard is generally the creator of shots for other players on the court, and Sue could not only create shots but take her own shots too, easily. That's why she's so good.

Sue is friends with everybody, she's so personable and engaging. She can have a conversation about anything, she's very charismatic, and people really warm to her. We are yin and yang—her personality is so out there, and she's vibrant, outgoing, she can talk to anybody, whereas I can be completely the opposite, especially so back then. We developed an incredible working partnership on the court, and off the court became good friends. On the court we complemented each other, and having the best point guard and a strong power forward makes it a hell of a lot easier to get the points for the team. A scorer still needs a point guard to get them the ball. I've always said that I don't think I would have managed to achieve all I did in the US without Sue being there all the way.

Sue and I became joint captains of Seattle after she was drafted. Coming through college she had plenty of experience with presentation, and the media, she's very articulate. Sue knew how to talk to them, how to tell them what they wanted to hear. I watched her that entire season and she was so good at it. Being around her made it easier for me in social situations, in dealing with the media, in everything, because she took up the slack. I watched and I learnt a lot from Sue.

The two of us went on to play in the All-Star games that season. I really didn't like the hype around them. It seemed like it was show time for nothing, an accolade really, and being in that environment used to make me feel quite ill, it was too overwhelming. An entire weekend and all we did was have photographs taken and pose, wear dressy clothes, sign autographs. Wearing high heels and dresses has never been my thing. I'm every part a woman and love all things feminine, what we do and how we do it, but dressing up like that was unusual for me, normally I would be wearing training gear, being myself. I'm a real comfort creature— anything *out* of my comfort zone I struggle with. I wish that I loved wearing dresses and glamming up more, but that's just not who I am. Now I'm older I'm a lot better at dealing with it than when I was young, but back then it felt like I was constantly being pushed into situations where I wasn't comfortable, wasn't being myself, and that wasn't the career I thought I'd chosen. Over there you're in the spotlight, here people have always sort of let me be who I am. In Australia I didn't have to worry, because all I had to do was play.

Seattle made it to the playoffs that year, and we came up against the LA Sparks. Lisa Leslie and I ignored each other completely, which had become the norm—except when we were on the court. In the second game, she kneed me in the groin and I came down hard. I managed to foul her three times in six minutes and ended up on the bench. I took everything so personally with her, every match up against Lisa just seemed to get more and more physical.

LA pushed us out of the playoffs in the first round and ended up beating New York Liberty to take out the 2002 final. When I was home in Australia after that season, I still had the niggling peroneal injury, but I'd also made a decision. I needed to be stronger. I started drinking protein shakes, and eating a lot more protein in my diet, together with lifting weights to build up muscle. I was determined— not only did I need to get bigger, I also needed to dominate in the key.

15

...

Changing of the Guard

I celebrated my 21st birthday twice in 2002. The first, just before the WNBA season in Canberra, with my friends from all over, at a party held at Tilley's. My second 21st was after the WNBA season had finished. My parents organised a party in Albury and all my family from Sydney came down, all my aunties and uncles who I'd grown up with, Mum and Dad's best friends, Tom Maher came down for it, anyone who was a special figure in my life was there, it was lovely.

After the WNBA season ended in August, I was back with the Opals and we travelled to China in September 2002 for the 14th FIBA World Championship. We'd taken bronze at the last world championships in Germany four years earlier, and were keen for another medal.

Jan Stirling had come in to replace Tom Maher as coach, and Timmsy, Robyn Maher and Shelley Sandie had all retired, there were plenty of new young faces in the team, it was a new era for the Opals, and for me. Tom had moved on from coaching the Opals, and was now coaching us at the Capitals, with Graffy taking a year-long sabbatical. I'd come through the Opals with Tom, I knew him. Jan was tough but in a different way from Tom, and we had a personality clash. I'd become well known in basketball, it was almost like, 'this is the new coach of the Australian team, and you've got this young superstar who thinks she knows best'. We had to get on, I wasn't going anywhere, and she'd just been appointed and she wasn't going anywhere, but it was a battle of wills.

Playing at the world championships was huge, but I was suffering from shin splint pain, which is common in athletes and is often caused by the tendons and muscles that run the length of the shin pulling on the bone and creating inflammation. I'd suffered with shin splints since I was a child and it was always rather painful. The best treatment is rest, but being in the Opals I still wanted to play on it. We beat Spain and Argentina, but in the game against Japan, Jan only had me on court for 13 minutes and I felt like she didn't have faith in me.

Brownie was Jan's assistant coach, and he organised a meeting with me and the other assistant coach to talk about what was going on. I was angry, I felt we'd had little preparation before the tournament as a team. I'd been in the

Opals five years and grown from a kid into a young woman, and all of a sudden, all the people who were closest to me had left. I don't think I realised at the time how much of an impact they had had on me, and I was finding that without Tom being there it was different, and I've always been resistant to change. Brownie calmed me down in that meeting, Jan was the coach and I had to work with her, whether I initially liked her decisions or not. So, I did. Some things aren't always perfect—our coach–player style was rocky at the start and only developed over time, but our personalities and friendship also developed, and by the end of it there was mutual respect. That's really all you can ask for in any professional relationship.

We made it through our first group with three straight wins and went on to play and beat Yugoslavia and China, before being beaten by the Olympic bronze medallists Brazil, by just one point. We still made the finals, where we downed France and were in the semis against the US. If we won, we would be in the final against either Russia or South Korea, depending who won their match. If we lost, we would be playing for bronze.

In the semi-final, we led twice by four points in the second quarter, and the American coach kept Sheryl Swoopes and Lisa Leslie on court for virtually the entire 40 minutes of the game. I was fouled out early, and three of us were playing with injuries, but we hung in there and gave them a scare, eventually losing by 15 points to earn the right to play Korea for the bronze. We then beat Korea by 31 points to take out bronze, the second time the Opals had won a medal at a world championship. I was named in the World All-Star team. Lisa Leslie was named MVP after the US won against Russia 79–74 and took the gold. I led the tournament with a 23.1 point average per game, my highest being 33 points in the game against France.

We came back to Australia, and started the 2002/2003 WNBL season. After returning from the world championships I'd had X-rays to try and understand my ongoing peroneal pain, only to find out that rather than just rolling my ankle in training six months earlier at the beginning of the WNBA season, I'd actually fractured it. Because it hadn't healed properly, it had started pulling on my fibula, the smaller bone in the lower leg, which had led to the stress fractures in my right leg. This wouldn't have happened if I'd rehabbed the ankle injury properly. Only rest would help cure it. Tom was coaching the Capitals, but on the eve of the first game against the Sydney Flames in early October, I was ordered to rest for three to four weeks so my injury could heal.

It was frustrating sitting out the first four games, and I really enjoyed playing again after the break. Tom complained in the media that I was being targeted, and at one point the referees were not calling fouls against me, but it wasn't going to slow the Caps down. We made it into the preliminary finals, to be played in Canberra against the Townsville Fire. We had a 16-point deficit in the first half and were still down nine points with five minutes remaining. I managed to score the next eight points, and we were trailing just two points with 20 seconds left when I made another shot for the basket. It went in but I was fouled by an opposition player. The score was level 67–67 as I went to the free-throw line. As I spun the ball in my hand I pictured myself shooting the perfect shot, and in my head I saw it float into the rim, I took the shot and it flew straight through. It was an incredible game, and I think I burst into tears after we won. It was a game to remember, I scored 38 points, had 21 rebounds and nine blocks, but everyone played well. We were straight into the finals, waiting to see who won the semi-final between Townsville and the Sydney Flames.

On a hot February afternoon, in a packed AIS arena, the final took place against the Flames. Sydney led by 12 points at half-time and it felt like Sydney had 'double teamed' me (put two defensive players on me instead of one) to try and slow me down, but that left openings for other players as they stepped up. At the start of the third quarter, after a succession of three-pointers, the Flames' lead blew out to 17 points, but the Caps turned that around with a 16–0 run to get us back into the game. The Flames had a two-point lead going into the fourth. With just five minutes left, we hit the lead for the first time since the third minute of the game, before Sydney downed a three-pointer, with just 80 seconds left. I shot a basket, and then Kristen got a free throw and we hit the lead, the score 68–66 before we fouled my fellow Opal and Sydney player Belinda Snell with just 2.7 seconds left, giving the Flames the opportunity to tie the game. Belinda only downed one of her free throws before Kristen was fouled and got a free throw, which she sank. Final score, Capitals 69, Flames 67. What a game. The Capitals had won their third WNBL title.

It was Tom's seventh WNBL title, he only coached the Capitals that one year, before becoming head coach of the New Zealand National Women's Basketball team. I took out my third WNBL MVP and was top scorer of the season. As winners of the WNBL in the 2002/2003 season, the Capitals were asked to play at the inaugural FIBA Women's World League, to be played in October 2003 between basketball clubs from around the world who'd all won their national championships. The Capitals were going to Russia after the next WNBA season.

16

...

Being Valued

I arrived back in Seattle to find that we had a new coach, Anne Donovan, and that my fellow Opal, Tully Bevilaqua, had joined the Storm, having played with the Cleveland Rockers and Portland Fire previously. Another Opal, Sandy Brondello, who'd become like a big sister to me after the Olympics, was also on the Seattle Storm team, and it made that time so much more fun.

By this time we'd all been introduced to the Kangaroo and Kiwi Bar in Seattle, owned by fellow Aussie Brad Howe from Harden-Murrumburrah in New South Wales. It was so much fun to walk in there on our afternoons off, or for after-game drinks, and just expect the beer to be flowing and the laughs to begin. We used to go there for every social gathering with teammates, friends and family, it became our natural hangout. Fans even started hanging out there, too, because they knew they'd catch a glimpse of all of us off the court letting our hair down. The Kangaroo and Kiwi Bar and Brad became a sanctuary for me in Seattle.

Anne, our new coach, had been a post player, a 4/5 player for the US national team, and was a two-time gold medal Olympian in the 1980s. Her arrival was a turning point in my basketball career. She worked with me individually and on a daily basis. She motivated me throughout the season, and that's what I wanted and needed to develop my inside game.

As a young player, you're always developing and you can always get better, but I think she got hold of me when I could get even stronger and bigger, and she was very willing to put the extra work into me. We'd train, and I'd either shoot or work with her before or after practice. I put on more weight and muscle, and she took a real interest in getting me inside the key more often in games. I think the Storm needed to do this, to help me become the player I could be, to become as dominant as I needed to be. Soon I started going 'into the paint'—inside the key—and being more of a physical presence there. Anne motivated me to be a better basketball player, just like Tom had.

The best coaches I ever had all did that for me, brought out my best. Gaining Anne's outside perspective and assistance in developing my skills was just what I needed, at that age I couldn't do it myself. In the US, it's not very common for a head coach to put that much time into a player, assistant coaches do a lot of that work, not so much a head coach. It paid off, because Anne became one of those coaches I wanted to be good for, and she made it fun.

Anne picked up pretty quickly that I wasn't good with flying, and we'd sit next to each other on planes and talk about basketball, talk about anything to distract me, and she became a good friend of mine. Friendships and relationships don't come easily to me. Like anyone, when you form friendships and alliances you need to start off feeling like you belong. I hadn't been able to form friendships early on in the Australian junior team, I was taken under the wing in the seniors, and now in my third year of living and playing in a foreign country I was starting to feel like I belonged there. Having Anne was a real turning point in my WNBA career.

Jenny Boucek, who was assistant coach of the Storm at the time, also became a good friend, and has remained so over the years. As well as Anne and Jenny, I had close friends around me on the team, like Sue Bird, Adia Barnes, Sandy and Tully. When I started forming bonds with people who were really important to me both on and off the court I started to feel comfortable at Seattle, and that was amazing.

That year I was again picked to play with the All-Star team. Midway through the season we were playing the LA Sparks, and all of Anne's hard work with me paid off, with personal career highs in scoring, rebounding, assists and field-goal percentages. I set a WNBA league record that game, with 17 successful field goals from 23 attempts, 13 rebounds and three blocks, and we handed the Sparks their biggest loss in franchise history, with LA going down 56 points to our 92. Fans started wearing white T-shirts to our games with 'LJ for MVP' stamped across the front, it was huge.

The MVP or Most Valuable Player in the WNBA is awarded at the end of each season, to the best player, voted on by a panel of national sportswriters and broadcasters, who are asked to select their top five choices for the award, with ten points being awarded for a first-place vote, seven for second, five for third, three for fourth and one for fifth. A MVP in the US is just a title, but it's like being labelled the world's best player. Even though there isn't such a thing, it's almost an assumption because of the high standard of the WNBA. The US media really beefed it up, relaying my stats, constantly comparing me with other players, and everyone in Seattle seemed to want me to win it. I'd played in three All-Star games by then, had been WNBA Player of the Week three times that season, averaged 21.2 points per game and 8.5 rebounds, had led the scoring, was fifth in rebounds and fourth in blocks, and had attained 1000 WNBA career points, the youngest in the league to do so. But no foreigner had ever taken out a WNBA MVP, and I was only 23. To further reduce my chances, despite some awesome games, Seattle didn't make it to the playoffs, with lots of player injuries throughout the season. All MVP recipients had at least made the playoffs.

Mum and Dad were in Seattle with me when the Storm didn't make the finals, helping me look at an apartment to buy. I was standing in this apartment when I received a phone call from the league and found out that I'd been awarded MVP of the league that year. I was in complete disbelief, I hugged Mum and I think I may have cried, and then I rang the three coaches I really respected, those who'd probably been the most influential in my career—Anne Donovan, Tom Maher and Phil Brown—to tell them personally. Anne certainly had been influential that season, Tom with the national team, and Brownie because I'd been a kid when he coached me at the AIS, he was such a good coach for developing young players. They'd instilled a lot of values in me as a player, a lot of skill development, demanded the best out of me at training, playing, everything, and I'd given it. When I got the MVP, I think I wanted to share it with those three coaches, because they'd put so much time into developing me as a player.

I'd effectively been recognised as the best player of the toughest league in the world. Despite my age, despite being a foreigner, I'd won. It was huge. A MVP wasn't something I focused on, as long as I trained hard enough and felt good about playing, then that was all that really mattered to me. But to Seattle and the fans, it was amazing. I didn't feel deep down that I deserved it, but that didn't matter, it was exciting and I was certainly caught up in it. Never in my wildest dreams did I think I would ever be good enough to win that award.

It was grounding to come back to Australia to play after all of that. I remember playing a stinking hot game in Penrith in 40 degree Celsius heat, which was nothing like playing in an airconditioned 20 000 seat stadium in the US. The Penrith stadium would have been lucky to seat 1000 and certainly wasn't airconditioned. It was still great being back, I loved it because it felt like the pressure was off, I could just get out there and play. I wanted to enjoy the game, and I think in some ways I'd stopped enjoying it—no matter where I played overseas, there were always little rivalries and power plays. It was just different here, it was like I was home to play, it was basketball. The tin shed stadiums were familiar to me, and more often than not once the game had ended I would be able to go and unwind with people I loved and cared about, in our beautiful summer heat. And as well as all this, especially back then, I was playing with my friends.

I had so much fun playing in the WNBL because I tended to dominate here—not because it wasn't hard, it *was* hard, and it was demanding, but it was home and it was a whole lot of fun. In the US, I had to psych myself up for every game. The emotional energy it took to prepare for games over there was just so draining. Playing back in Australia was always good for me. I would have stayed in Australia my whole career if the money had been here to earn a living, to earn enough to put savings aside for life after basketball. But then, would I have become the player I did? Going to live and play in the US pushed me out of my comfort zone, gave me the opportunity to work with people like Anne.

The WNBL season started in October that year and our first game was against the Perth Lynx. I was on fire, having fun, landing 48 points and 18 rebounds in my 30 minutes on the court. We beat them 102–65. The Canberra Capitals then all flew to Russia to play our FIBA Women's World League obligation, which was basically like a world club championship, where the top teams from the top basketball leagues all over the world came together to compete for the title.

17

...

Ekaterinburg

Select teams from all over the world had been asked to the FIBA Women's World League, and Graffy had returned to the Canberra Capitals as our coach after her sabbatical. We flew Qantas to Japan and then had to fly Aeroflot over to Moscow. I'd only ever heard bad things about the Russian airline, which certainly didn't help my apprehension about flying. The flight to Russia was thankfully fine, we arrived in Moscow and then we had to get on a Samara Airlines plane for the last leg. The Samara Airlines plane had a glass nose on it like a military bomber, and the interior had purple velvet on the walls, the seats were folded totally forward, the windows had mini curtains on them, and cabin luggage could be stashed anywhere. I honestly felt real foreboding actually getting into that plane, let alone flying in it. We landed in Samara, and one of these same planes was sitting on the tarmac, the glass in the bomber nose at the front of the plane had all been shattered and the engine looked like it had just fallen off and had been left lying on the ground—and I later found out that that's exactly what had happened. We were there playing and I spent the entire time frightened out of my mind about getting on one of those planes and flying back to Moscow, I was focused on that thought and the resulting fear almost the entire time. When I play I just play, but only being on the court two to three hours a day meant the rest of the time I was thinking about the engine lying on the tarmac, and I didn't enjoy that thought one bit.

We lined up against one of the two Russian teams. I later found out that Graffy, who was sitting on the bench as we were warming up, was apparently approached by a Russian man who said, 'You know to lose'. Graffy was like, 'What?', and he repeated his statement and walked away, but because of his thick accent it didn't really register with her. This same Russian man, Shabtai Kalmanovich, made himself known to me after the game.

As it turned out, the score was pretty close anyway, but ultimately we couldn't match up with that Russian team. UMMC Ekaterinburg had so many foreigners, including DeLisha Milton, Sheryl Swoopes and two other top American players, and it was a really good Russian squad, which included half the Russian national team. We came fifth in the competition. CSKA Moscow managed to beat the American WNBA team, with Ekaterinburg coming third, but I was top scorer of the tournament.

After the tournament Shabtai Kalmanovich called my agent at the time, Robyn Danzey, and told her, 'I'll pay US$100 000 for Lauren to play for a month in playoffs and finals with Ekaterinburg, if you fly over here'—$100 000, for one month? You don't knock that back.

■ ■ ■

The Caps had come fourth in the WNBL, and I'd missed seven games in the middle of the 2003/2004 WNBL season with the recurring stress fractures in my shins, but still managed to take out Season MVP and top scorer. Our season ended with a surprising semi-final loss to Adelaide in February 2004, and by April I was heading over to play in the Russian Super League finals for Shabtai. Mum came with me to Ekaterinburg. There were statues of Lenin, a beautiful big cathedral—the 'Cathedral on the Blood'—it was the city where the last Tsar and his family were executed, there is so much history there.

Shabtai flew us over first class, and it was amazing, so much room. When you're tall like Mum and myself, folding ourselves into economy seats for long periods of time is always a struggle. Mum loved it, we didn't even feel like we were in a plane, it certainly helped with my anxiety, especially after four or five glasses of French champagne before we even took off.

We arrived at Sheremetyevo International Airport in Moscow at night. Shabtai's people picked us up in a car and drove us in a motorcade to a private airport on the other side of the city, where there was a private plane to take us to Ekaterinburg. We even had a police escort. Shabtai really put it all on, we were racing through the streets, and I was thinking, 'This is ridiculous, this is larger than life!'. Why did we have to speed through Moscow to get to a private jet that couldn't wait an extra half an hour? That was a bit nerve-racking, but we made it on to the plane and flew to Ekaterinburg, although I didn't end up playing that much at all.

In my first game, Shabtai was sitting on the bench next to me and Mum when there was a foul called by the referee. Shabtai was furious, he got up and walked on to the court and started abusing the ref, and amazingly he didn't get ejected. He just walked on to the court and abused the official. It was a grand final series in a Russian league game, but they didn't eject him from the stadium like they would in the US or Australia, he still stayed on the bench after that. Mum and I turned and looked at the exchange between Shabtai and the ref, and then at each other, and just started laughing, it was ridiculous. But it wasn't a joke, that was the man, that was Shabtai and the sort of power he had.

With memories of Samara Airlines, I asked Shabtai to get me on the train because I simply didn't want to fly. I preferred being on one of their old trains with a little cabin to being on a Russian plane. Mum had been really excited about getting on a charter jet and having champagne, big leather seats and leg room, and I had to tell her we were going on a train trip, Dr Zhivago style. I thought it was quite lovely being on the train and settling into a nice cosy little cabin. But Mum loves the big stuff. I don't, I'm not into the glitz and glamour and I think I'd experienced it often enough that it wasn't special anymore, it took too much out of me. Mum absolutely hated that trip on the train, the beds weren't big enough, it was a poky cabin, it took too long. She hated it, but I felt safer.

Mum flew back to Australia, and I went back to Moscow, because Shabtai had invited me back to his office, he wanted to show me where he worked and lived. Once again, my motorcade was escorted to his office. When we arrived, we were let through boom gates guarded by what looked like military men, with great big AKs on their shoulders, and I thought, 'This is weird for an office'. I was escorted through the building to see him. When I got there he had a man with him, Shabtai stating by way of introduction that 'This is my Chechnyan brother'. I don't know what that guy's name was, I don't want to remember what his name was, he was a scary-looking guy and I remember not wanting to be there. I kept thinking it was all so bizarre, all these armed men hanging around the office in army camouflage gear.

Shabtai was a bit of an enigma to me really. He had an incredible sense of self. His office was full of gold, beautiful gold objects, frames, game boards, everything, like an artefact museum. He also had a bank in his office—behind this massive piece of artwork sat a huge safe with what seemed like every denomination of money inside. It was over the top and impressive, even though I don't think he was trying to impress, that was just the person he was.

I was lucky to play eight minutes a game on that visit to Ekaterinburg. I didn't realise it at the time, but the fact I was playing for Shabtai meant that if I ever played in Europe, it was going to be under him. I effectively belonged to him.

18

■ ■ ■

The Athens Dream

Before going to the US for the 2004 WNBA season, I'd been asked by the magazine *Black + White Photography* to pose for a special edition book, *The Athens Dream*, leading up to the Athens Olympics. They'd asked me to pose for an earlier edition but I'd said no, because I wasn't ready or comfortable enough with my body to be photographed naked. I'd always been the sort of kid who would have communal showers in a bathing suit. When they asked again a couple of years later, I thought long and hard about it. I agreed, and as with everything, I told Mum and asked her opinion. Both of my parents were really supportive, they may have had some doubts, which I totally understood, but as always left the decision ultimately up to me. I had this moment where I thought 'I'm going to do it', and pushed myself to commit. But then almost immediately after, I hugged Mum and thought, 'Why did I say yes?'. I'd agreed, I just had to talk myself into it, I could do it!

It's funny to think about it now, but when I was young I got this tattoo on the bottom of my foot, and I had to hide it from my parents, Dad was really against them. One day, when I was lying down in the living room with bare feet, he saw the tattoo and just about had a conniption. He said to me, 'Someone's going to take a photo of that one day', and I told him, 'I don't care'. But he was really upset about this stupid little tattoo. It felt like my mum and dad were worried about everything, and looking back, I know I was a rather eccentric young woman, I still am—I definitely have my own flow, but you only live once, right? Over the years, it just reached the point where both my parents would tell me that they loved me, supported me, and if I asked them for their opinion they'd tell me, they still do. But ultimately, it's my life.

When I arrived the morning of the photo shoot I immediately asked whether anyone had a bottle of champagne, or anything alcoholic, something I could drink to relax. It was a male photographer, I'd never met him before, there were another couple of people in the room and I felt really awkward, but I got through it, like I do everything, and the photos are truly beautiful.

I was able to choose the photos they used, and I was lucky enough to be on the front cover of one of the editions. The photos are truly stunning. There were a few shots in the book where I was really exposed, and I was worried what my parents would think, but they were really supportive. Mum and Dad loved the finished product. After Dad saw it for the first time he called me and told me he was proud of me—needless to say I still felt a little bit uneasy knowing my dad had seen the pictures.

Thirty-five Australian Olympic athletes posed for *The Athens Dream*, with its beautiful tasteful photographs of incredible athletic bodies, beautifully captured. I'd never do it again, because my body doesn't look like that anymore, but not only for that reason, I just don't feel the need to expose myself like that again. I felt totally liberated the day after that photo shoot, I felt beautiful and strong, particularly after I saw the pictures.

My nan was getting older, both my grandmothers were, but Mum's mum, Nanna Bennie, became seriously ill and Mum retired from work to take care of her. Mum and I are close as anything, and I missed her when I went back to the US, but she was busy looking after Nan.

With the Athens Olympics coming up, the WNBA season was going to be long, starting in May, breaking for a month for the Olympics, and then finishing up in October. I arrived for pre-season training in April and articles started appearing in the Seattle papers about *The Athens Dream* in June. It was relatively uncontroversial in Australia, but it created a stir in the US. The week the book was released over there, my player profile page on the WNBA website had 70 000 hits, a 3300 per cent increase from the week before. Not a lot of female athletes had posed nude over there at that time, and it was right on the back of my MVP win. Some people in the US, women in particular, saw it as attention-seeking. There were comments that if you're a woman in sport you have to get naked to gain attention. It wasn't that at all. It was both Australian men and women, Olympics athletes, posing for those pictures. I thought it was beautiful, very artsy, displaying amazing bodies. We put so much effort and time into creating these bodies so they can perform, why not show them off?

There was a bit of negativity in the US, but there was also a lot of positivity. Even last time I visited, someone asked me to sign a copy of the book, people still bring them out and get me to sign them. I never did any book signings in Australia, but in the US I think we had two, and there were a lot of people there. The publishers in Australia had to ship books to Seattle, with the money going to charity, there was simply nothing like that in the US at the time. Some people thought it brave, I thought it was worth it. I was definitely out of my comfort zone posing for those photos, but oddly enough that's often when I do the most rewarding things in my life—when I'm a little bit uncomfortable.

I really did the photo shoot thinking of an Australian audience, here it's quite prestigious to be asked. But in the US they saw it differently. Tully summed it up beautifully when she spoke with the American media in Seattle, 'The human body is nothing to be ashamed of'. But perhaps that's an Australian cultural thing, not an American one.

By the Olympic break at the beginning of August the Storm had won 17 of their 25 games played in the Western Conference, and I headed back to Australia to train with the Opals.

The Opals' first big tournament leading up to the Olympics was the FIBA Diamond Ball, which from 2000 to 2008 was held each Olympic year just prior to the Olympics. The first tournament had been for men's teams only, but 2004 and 2008 were for both men and women. Despite the US women's team being the then-reigning world champions, they didn't compete. We played in Greece and won, beating China in the finals 74–70, with Brazil coming in third. It was a great start to our 2004 Olympic campaign, we felt ready.

19

...

Athens Olympics

The Athens Olympics opening ceremony was on 13 August 2004, and we played our first match the following day, where we beat Nigeria 85–73, and I had a game high of 27 points. The Nigerian team had an American coach in Athens, and they never quit, coming within seven points with two minutes remaining, but we dug deep and defended their attack. At the other end of the court, the ball made it to me, and I managed to sink the last three buckets, all turn-around jump shots, where I'd post up back to the basket, someone would pass me the ball and I'd turn around and shoot over the defence.

Following that match we were up against world number two, Russia. Penny Taylor had a brilliant game for us and we won 75–56. We went on to consecutive wins over the other teams in our group, against Japan and host nation Greece. The match against Greece was Rachael Sporn's 300th game. There was a passionate home crowd cheering their team on, but we had plenty of Aussie support in the stands as well, and we silenced the Greek supporters early on as we took the lead.

Next, we played Brazil. We wanted to finish on top of our pool, but we'd lost to Brazil at the 2002 world championships in the last round by one point, before taking the bronze. In Athens we took out that game 84–66, we were at the top of our pool, but the US had also reached the top of their pool undefeated. Next, in the quarterfinals, we met New Zealand, who Tom Maher was now coaching. I'd strained a ligament in my ankle in the game against Brazil, but played on. We won 94–55 and were matched again against Brazil in the semis, a much closer game, which we won 88–75. We were in the gold medal match, against the US, again.

Mum and Dad weren't going to come to Athens originally because Nan was so sick, but when it looked like we might vie for that gold medal, my parents flew over at the very last minute, thanks to our beautiful Opals manager Marion 'Maz' Stewart. She's just a dream that woman, best manager I ever had.

We were getting ready to play in the gold medal match, but before our game Russia and Brazil were playing for the bronze medal. Russia won, and Shabtai, whose wife Anna was the captain of the Russian team at the time, was sitting on the team bench. This is in the 2004 Olympics, I don't know why he was on the bench of the Russian national team, he's not a coach, and he certainly wasn't a player, I truly have no idea how he got that pass, but he did. There is a strict 'no alcohol' rule at all of the Olympic venues, but when Russia won the bronze medal Shabtai pulled out this massive bottle of champagne and popped it on the court, just as we were about to go out and warm up for our match. It was unbelievable, but so typical of him. I remember that when we were warming up for the gold medal game our shoes were sticking to the floor because of the champagne.

It was Sue Bird's first Olympics, and she didn't play the final match. She was the rookie point guard for the US team, playing behind Dawn Staley and Shannon Johnson, who were rounding out their careers as two of the best point guards to play the game. Sue was soon to take that mantle, but it wasn't quite her time then—the US have an 'earn your stripes' mentality, it's very rare for a youngster to come into the team at their first Olympics and play huge minutes. Competing against a teammate can be hard, and it was always difficult playing against her because we had such a great partnership at the Storm. When we did play against each other, I think we both had times where we would call each other's name, forgetting we were on opposing teams. We always kept it as professional as possible, but it's really difficult with a tight friendship like that, there were moments where I would want to have a joke with her. There was one game where she was knocked down and I went and helped her up, because I cared about her and it was just natural. I didn't agree when people on my team said, 'You shouldn't do that'—well, no, above all she is one of my closest friends.

I was a starter for that gold medal match, with Suzy Batkovic, Trish Fallon our captain, Kristi Harrower and Penny Taylor, against the US starters Lisa Leslie, Sheryl Swoopes, Tamika Catchings and Tina Thompson. They simply outplayed us and we lost 63–74, but it felt like we were closer to beating them than we had been in Sydney. The closest we got was in the third quarter, when we were only one point behind. The US had another Olympic gold medal in women's basketball, we had our second Olympic silver.

Mum and Dad sat down with me after that game and explained that Nanna Bennie was about to pass away. They told me that I could either come home with them or go back to the WNBA, and for whatever reason I decided to go back to the WNBA, and instantly regretted it. As soon as I got to Seattle I thought, 'I can't do this, I have to go home!'. My coach Anne Donovan's reaction was 'What are you doing? You decided to come back here and we're about to vie for a championship', but I realised I needed to go back and say goodbye to my nan. To her credit Anne agreed, although I don't think she was happy about it, but I flew straight home and got to see Nan for a couple of days, it was one of the best decisions I ever made.

My mum and my nan have been such a huge part of my life. When I was visiting in the hospital, Nan was drifting in and out of consciousness quite a bit, and I started talking with my uncles, Mum's three brothers who were all there, and one of them asked me when I was going back to the US. Nan woke up and said, 'Don't talk about that! She's not going back'. It did make me feel sad about having to leave, but I think it hit Mum more, she still talks about it to this day. I had to return to the US, Seattle were in with a real chance at the championships and I couldn't let them down again. I felt a responsibility, it was my job, and they were my friends, I wanted to win for my teammates, our coaches and the Seattle community.

20

...

Day of the Storm

Seattle were in the playoffs, for only the second time, having been knocked out in the first round of the Western Conference by the LA Sparks just two years before. That year, the playoff rounds, the conference finals and then the WNBA final were the best of three games.

Nanna passed away in the first round of playoffs. That was really difficult, I was so sad, and playing when someone you love dies is the hardest. I talked to my coach Anne, and Mum and Dad, about going back to Albury for the funeral. Everyone at the Storm left the decision up to me, but Mum and Dad told me to stay and play.

When Nan died, we were in the first round against the Minnesota Lynx. We won that first game 70–58 and needed a second win to progress. The second game was the day before Nan's funeral, and I wore a black arm band in her honour and wrote 'Nanna B' on my Nikes so I thought of her every time I looked down. I know she was watching over me. Sue was sent off early with a broken nose in the first half after colliding with a Minnesota player. When Betty Lennox got into foul trouble, Anne brought Tully in as point guard and she added nine points, the crowd chanting her name repeatedly. With only ten minutes left we were down three points, I scored 18 points for the game, and with three minutes left to go we were ten points ahead—we held it and won 64–54. We'd made it through the first round, first time through for the Seattle Storm. Sue's nose was still bleeding at the end of the game, and she told us that it didn't hurt, but she was just being tough, her nose was on the other side of her face!

Dad somehow organised a video link through the local computer shop in Albury so I could watch Nan's funeral from Seattle that afternoon. One of my teammates, Sheri Sam, sat up and watched the funeral with me in a private office at the Seattle Storm headquarters. She was so supportive, it was hard being on the other side of the world at such a sad time for my family, and Sheri just held me and was there for me. That year in particular at Seattle there was a group of us who were really close. It was most of the team to be honest, Sue Bird, Tully, Adia Barnes, Sheri Sam, they were all like sisters.

The Western Conference final games were next. We were playing against the Sacramento Monarchs, who'd downed the LA Sparks two games to one in their round. Sue was wearing a face guard to try and protect her broken nose, and even though you could see her eye sockets were bruised purple and she was still badly swollen around her nose, she played on. It was a tight game, we went into overtime with each team on 72 points, and then the right-handed DeMya Walker from the Monarchs flipped up an awkward left-handed scoop shot and we all held our breath as the ball slowly teetered around and around the rim, almost falling out before tumbling through the middle, and they won by just two points. Two games left to win if we were going to make it through.

In the second game Sue was still playing in her face mask—she was due to have surgery on her broken nose the day before our third game, but she was determined to play. We won the second game 66–54 at home.

Sue had a blinder of a game in the third match after her surgery, we all did. I managed to drop all five three-pointers in the second half and we won 82–62. The Seattle Storm were going to the WNBA finals for the first time, against the Eastern Conference winner Connecticut Sun. The city of Seattle was ecstatic, the media, the fans, it felt like the entire city was behind us, we had a chance to make history.

The first game was in Connecticut, and they won by four points. Their defence was too strong. We had two more games to come back and win. The next game was at our home ground, Seattle's KeyArena, in front of a crowd of over 17 000 people, it was an amazing atmosphere. We led the whole game and with four minutes left had a six-point lead, but anything can happen in four minutes. The Sun scored five points in the final 90 seconds of the game, and called time out with just 3.1 seconds remaining. When we went back out, the Connecticut forward Nykesha Sales evaded me, got open and tried for a three-pointer. It was my fault, and I remember watching the ball fly through the air almost in slow motion and thinking, 'Nan, if you're here please don't let her make this shot'. She'd scored so many points that game, she was on fire, and for whatever reason that shot hit the corner of the backboard and didn't go in, the game was over. Talk about a sigh of relief. We won 67–65. One game each. The decider would again be at KeyArena, two days later.

Every seat was filled in the stadium for the third game, fans wearing yellow and green wigs, face paint, homemade signs, it was incredible. The Sun had made the mistake of trying to take Sue and me out, and the other Storm players all stepped up. Betty Lennox had an unbelievable finals series, but the last game of the series was epic. Just before the final buzzer, the crowd in KeyArena were chanting 'Betty, Betty, Betty', and she rightly took out the MVP for the final. The final score—Connecticut 60, Seattle 74. The stadium was packed to the rafters. They measured the noise level when we won that game and it was apparently louder than a Boeing 747 taking off.

Anne became the first female coach to win a WNBA final, and the Storm became only the third professional sports team in the city of Seattle's history to win a national title in any sport. It was unbelievable, we had a ticker-tape parade through Seattle a couple of days after, on what the mayor called 'Storm Day', that's the sort of stuff they do for all teams over there. The city was abuzz. Tully and I stayed in Seattle and partied and had fun for days, it was great. Seattle really embraced our team, they loved us, still do. Seattle will always have that team because the community loves the girls, the team and the WNBA. That's one thing I'll always remember about Seattle, how the city embraced me as a player, a person, as well as the team as a whole.

21

...

Shot Ankle

Back in 2002, when I'd rolled my right ankle badly at training and unwittingly gone on to play on the fracture, I'd developed stress fractures in my fibula. The injury had continued to bother me, and now the ligaments in that ankle were shot.

I decided to play through it at the Olympics and in the WNBA finals, there was no time out for surgery, and in the end it was just unbearable. Honestly, you get used to pain, but with the constant flying and swelling of my ankle, my ligaments were so loose after the WNBA that I'd be walking down the street and my ankle would just go out from under me causing more damage each time.

Playing basketball, we'd all get lots of injuries that we considered pretty minor, a sprain or a pulled muscle or ligament. Even though they cause a lot of pain at the time, you don't think it's doing any harm, so you suck it up and play through it, and I got used to playing through most things. Most injuries do get better, but when they don't and you're not recovering and everything else starts to break down around it, it needs to be looked at, to be fixed, your body is trying to tell you something.

When I returned to Australia they found more damage than was initially thought, I'd fractured my ankle and I had bone spurs at the back of my ankle that were causing some trouble. At the age of 23, it could have been another career-ending injury. That November, I went in for a complete ankle reconstruction, an arthroscope and a posterior clearance—where they tried to remove all the bone chips—and I was told that I'd be off the court for three to four months. That put an end to returning to the Capitals that season, and I was contemplating taking a whole year off, spending time with my family and friends and not going back to Seattle. As I was off contract, there was no obligation to return.

■ ■ ■

Following *The Athens Dream* photo shoot, I'd been asked to do an American *Sports Illustrated* feature, a swimsuit shoot on a Miami beach. In January 2005, the middle of the American winter, Mum travelled with me to Miami.

It was a free trip, they flew us business class and it was fun to be able to share that with her. We were there for three days, and although the shoot was for only one of those days it took all day, about seven hours.

They picked us up at six in the morning and took us to a mobile home on a beautiful secluded beach on the Florida Keys, and it was freezing. I kept thinking 'What am I doing?'. But ultimately it turned out to be a beautiful sunny day. I really enjoyed doing it, it was something different, there was no pressure, all I had to do was pose and have my photo taken in various swimsuits—that was until they asked me to take my bikini top off and cover my breasts with my forearms. I did it, and it was a lovely picture, although now I would say no! But back then, posing for that photo shoot was nothing like the pressure I felt going out on a basketball court in front of thousands of people.

I really didn't take any notice of the publicity. In the US, the magazine was published not long after the shoot, but it came out later in Australia and the reaction at home was pretty good I think. If there was any negative feedback I wasn't aware of it. It's all part of my coping mechanism though—if I think something is controversial, I don't read newspapers, if we lose games, I won't go and read the match report. Self-Preservation 101.

We came back to Australia and I kept rehabilitating my ankle, going to the physio three times a week, doing cross-training, bike riding, and my ankle was slowly feeling better. Anne Donovan had been in touch, and the Storm wanted me back. They negotiated with my agent at the time and by then I really wanted to get back into my basketball after a few months off court. I signed up for a 34-game, three-month season, and flew over to the US to train for the season starting in May.

The Capitals also got in touch before I left. I'd missed the 2004/2005 season, but they wanted me to sign up for the 2005/2006 season, which I did, my ankle felt better and I'd always loved playing with the Capitals.

That year my great friend Suzy Batkovic was drafted number 22 in the WNBA, with Seattle picking her up. We'd played in the juniors together, and gone through the AIS together, played in the Gems and Opals, and taken silver together at Athens, and it was good to have her with us at the Storm. Tully had decided to stay in Australia to play with the Capitals that year.

2004 had been a pretty tough year, losing Nanna and then playing in Australia, Russia, Greece at the Olympics and in the US, before coming back to Australia for the ankle surgery. But in the 2005 WNBA season I had another type of health scare.

After a regular health check, I was diagnosed with pre-cancerous cervical cells. I made an appointment with a gynaecologist, I had to get another Pap smear to confirm that it was pre-cancer, and that diagnosis kind of scared the bejesus out of me. Sports injuries are one thing, but cancer was a whole new unknown area. I had to undergo a procedure to have it removed, and that whole process really scared me. It was one of those things that I hadn't really wanted to share with anyone because I didn't fully understand it myself, so I don't think I coped well with it, but was glad Suzy was there, she was a great support. I think I missed a trip with the Storm because of the procedure, but thankfully was right after that.

After winning the WNBA finals the previous year, Seattle made it to the playoffs again in 2005, but we were beaten two games to one by Sheryl Swoopes' team, the Houston Comets, in the first round, with Sheryl taking out the WNBA MVP award. That entire season the same hype was happening around me, with the possibility of my second MVP in 2005. I'd managed to gain the most top votes, but Sheryl scored more third and fourth votes, edging me out by the narrowest of margins, two votes, 327 to 325.

My ankle had been hurting again, even after the surgery, but as usual I'd been taking medication, and I'd played through the pain all season. I was back home getting ready to play with the Canberra Capitals again in the WNBL when I found out about missing out on the WNBA MVP by only two points. Apparently, I told my dad that I was a little disappointed, but I hadn't had any real expectations of winning another title. Knowing I was that close to having another MVP in a league like that still blows me away, but I wasn't upset. Sheryl is a great player, one of the best of all time, she was always lovely and kind to me, and she was also the best number two guard the women's game had seen at that time, she was so deserving of that award.

SHOT ANKLE

■ ■ ■

I started back with the WNBL for the 2005/2006 season, and was looking forward to playing in Australia, but by October, after just two games, the dreaded shin splints returned. I was experiencing a sharp pain through my left shin, and my lower leg was swollen. I'd played through shin soreness for years, but now the pain had become unbearable. Stress fractures were such frustrating injuries for me because I'd always had shin pain, and had tried to manage them with ice and massage. But they'd become so bad that I couldn't sleep at night, and there was nothing I could do about it. I couldn't even walk up the stairs at home. I had scans and found new major stress fractures through my left tibia, a major weight-bearing bone in my lower leg, but I couldn't actually pinpoint when the fracture had occurred. It hadn't been an issue when I was playing, painkillers before every game always masked the worst of the pain. Initially I was told that I would be out of the game for months and would require a rod through my tibia, because the two cracks in my shin connected with each other. Naturally I was scared, but fortunately that wasn't the case and I only required eight weeks out of the game with rehab and physio. I was told to rest, no jumping, no running.

There is nothing worse than being in top physical condition and feeling like you are playing the best you've ever played, and then having to sit on the bench. But I took the

141

medical advice seriously, and stopped playing in the WNBL for nearly two months. It was just a really annoying cycle of injuries, for me, my teammates and my coaches.

My shoulder, my ankle and now the shin fracture—I of course thought the worst, what if one of these injuries actually ended my career? At 24, I realised I had no formal education, I had nothing to fall back on, and that thought really hit home. I needed a qualification, and while I was rehabilitating, I had time. I hadn't been able to study well in high school, I was constantly and easily distracted, but I decided to enrol in a diploma of Business Management course by correspondence. Partway through I realised that I'd found a way of studying that worked for me, I could read through the books, concentrate, understand and get it done, by myself, in my own time, with no distractions. I proved to myself that I could study, and that was really satisfying.

The AIS were great. Instead of on-court training, I'd train in a pool, use an exercise bike, anything to reduce pressure on my shins. Thankfully it hadn't been a career-ending injury, but it was still one that needed to be rehabilitated properly, and this time I was determined to do just that. I still wanted to play on for another eight, ten years or more, but to make that happen I realised I had to manage my body better.

I missed the Opals' December training camp, and although I felt frustrated I was equally determined to make the 18th Commonwealth Games in Melbourne in March 2006. Basketball isn't played at every Commonwealth Games, it's up to the discretion of the host country. Australia had successful men's and women's basketball teams, so of course the sport was included. I was going to play, I wanted to play for my country.

After taking 13 weeks off to rehabilitate my shins, and not being allowed to train more than 20 to 30 minutes a day, I returned to the Capitals in January for the last four games of the season. My first game back showed how unfit I actually was, with Graffy only putting me on to the court for 20 minutes of the total game, and we lost to the Sydney Flames 54–52. We won two of the next three games, and were placed third on the ladder behind Adelaide and the Dandenong Rangers as we headed into the finals. We managed to make the grand final by beating the Bulleen Boomers 67–62, and then Adelaide by two points in overtime, and were lined up to play Dandenong. It was a credit to the whole team that the Caps were into yet another WNBL championship. Katrina Hibbert took out the Season MVP, the Capitals won their fourth championship in seven years, beating Dandenong 68–55, and I was awarded the Finals MVP. Winning is the best cure for any injury.

22

...

Commonwealth Games

Preparations for the 2006 Commonwealth Games were heating up and there were still concerns about my shins, but I was playing. I was named not only in the Opal line-up but also as joint captain with 'Harley', Jenny Whittle. Captaining the national team was wonderful, I felt really honoured—the Australian team was such a huge part of my career and my life, it had always been very important to me. I'd been with the Opals nine years, and along with Harley was probably the most experienced player on the team, and to co-captain with her was fantastic.

We played the first game against India and won by 100 points, 146–46. We were ranked number two in the world, India number 41, and we had both size and experience over them. It felt good to get a decent run up and down the court, playing 20 minutes of the game and downing 41 points.

We followed with wins against Mozambique, England and Nigeria, and we were straight through to the gold medal match against the New Zealand Tall Ferns, in front of a huge crowd. Before our game we watched the bronze medal match between England and Nigeria, with England taking the bronze 78–75. The Tall Ferns were a very physical team, but in the grand final we pulled ahead on points and won gold for Australia 77–39. That victory felt better than winning a WNBL or WNBA championship or any MVP award—we'd won gold in our own country. I couldn't see the chance of playing for gold again in Australia. At the end of the game I was handed an Australian flag, and the whole team jumped and danced around the arena. It felt very special.

The Commonwealth Games women's basketball final took place on 23 March, two days before the Games finished, but I missed the closing ceremony. Less than 24 hours after our gold medal win, I was back home in Albury, playing basketball in the stadium I'd grown up in, as a guest player for the first game of the newly formed Lady Bandits. Dad had played in the men's team, the Bandits, which had started the year after I was born, and I'd grown up watching them play, but the Lady Bandits had been formed just six months earlier, in 2005, and were due to play their first game in the South East Australian Basketball League (SEABL). Dad had played a really big part in getting a women's team up and running in Albury, he was president of the men's

Albury SEABL team at the time, and I'd been asked to play a one-off game. Ray Tomlinson, my old coach from the junior team, had agreed to coach the Lady Bandits, and there was an incredible buzz in Albury and at the sports stadium that night. I'd been given a special light-blue number 15 jersey to wear, and whenever I played in that stadium over the years, I felt so much support and pride. That day all the people I'd grown up with, played with, my Albury friends and family, were there to support me and the new team.

■ ■ ■

Less than two weeks after the Commonwealth Games, we were hosting the Opals' World Challenge, with games between the Opals, the US, China and Chinese Taipei. We won in Cairns against China, but I didn't play as I was ill with a virus. After every big tournament I tended to come down with a flu—I got sick when I stopped, it was just one of those things. I only played part of the game against Chinese Taipei, which we also won, but I wanted to be at full strength to play against the US. My Seattle coach Anne Donovan was coaching the US team, and we lost that first game against them in Cairns by 20 points, 83–63. Our next match would be in Canberra, and after winning gold in our own country just weeks before, we beat the US for the first time in an official international tournament, 76–65, at the

AIS arena. It was always special beating the US, because it didn't happen very often, let alone in front of a home crowd. I don't think losing meant much to them, but we were elated, and to achieve the win in Canberra was the best. It was a great ending to the Opals' World Challenge, a huge match for the girls, for me, for Canberra, for Australia. We'd done it. We'd beaten the US.

Looking back, it was the perfect way to thank all the Capitals fans and the people who'd supported me in Canberra. I needed to say thanks, because I was leaving the WNBL. I'd signed another playing contract with Seattle, but also a contract in South Korea. I'd play the WNBA for the Storm from May until August, then go to the world championships in September with the Opals, and then play in South Korea each December for the next three years.

■ ■ ■

I arrived back in Seattle and began the 2006 WNBA season. Our third match was against Phoenix, where I scored a career-high 35 points and nine rebounds—I was back playing my best. But as we played the regular season, my left shin started giving me trouble again. I kept playing, using medication to get through, eventually having to sit out a game towards the end of the season. I made the All-Star team for the fifth time, and on the tenth anniversary of the

WNBA was named in the All-Decade team, together with Lisa Leslie, Sheryl Swoopes and Sue Bird. I was once again the youngest, and the only foreigner. We were honoured in the middle of our last All-Star game against the Eastern Conference team at Madison Square Garden in New York, but the pain was like a knife going through my left shin whenever I ran, and I had to sit out the second half of the game, and the two last games of the season.

Seattle made the playoffs and were pitted against Los Angeles for the Western Conference semi-finals, but the Storm were knocked out, by two games to one. I stayed in Seattle and rehabbed my shin, and met up with our Opals girls at Raleigh–Durham, North Carolina, for preparation games against the US. The 15th FIBA World Championship was held in Brazil, and I only had a month to rehab my shin fractures, again restricting my training to the pool and an exercise bike. I had to get better, I wasn't ready to leave the sport yet, and after taking two bronze medals at the 1998 and 2002 world championships, I wanted another medal for my country.

That world championship in Brazil was huge. We won against every team in our group—Canada, Senegal, Spain, Brazil and Argentina—before winning the quarterfinal against France 79–66. We were matched up against Brazil for the semi to earn a place in the gold medal game, and were in the crowd watching the other decider for the gold medal between the US and Russia. We'd been trying to get ourselves psyched-up for this inevitable game against the

US, expecting the same old battle if we made it through.

At half-time Russia were up, and I remember thinking, 'Yeah, this won't last'. It came to three-quarter time, Russia were still up and we were actually saying to each other, 'This won't last'. And then, at the end of the fourth quarter, Russia had won. We were stunned. We were going into a gold medal game without having to take on the US, for the first time ever. It was amazing, Russia had beaten them. When we met Brazil in the semi there was just this hyped feeling in the Opals as we played, and when we took that match 66–57 we felt like we'd won the championship before we'd even had the final game.

We went back to the motel and I called a team meeting, the Opals needed to go out and win this gold medal. All of the girls came back to the room I was sharing with Tully. We had a chat about it, how we were going to cope with the pre-game excitement, how not having to play the US was affecting us—we were all completely blown away.

In that final match, Russia took an early 9–2 lead, but we went on a 17–5 run to finish the first quarter and established a lead they never came close to, eventually winning the match 91–74. We had won the FIBA World Championship, the Opals had won gold at a world championship for the first time.

Harley retired after the 2006 world championship. She'd actually retired after the 2002 world championship, but Tom convinced her to come back following the Athens Olympics. Harley's amazing, she's a great player and a great person. She'd known me from the time I'd joined the Opals as a teenager. I'd been an aggressive young thing, and I think being just a kid and not physically strong enough to battle against older players like Harley, there'd been some elbows thrown out between us—I know I annoyed the hell out of her, but she's such a good person, and great fun.

It had been an incredible 2006, topped off by my induction into the AIS Hall of Fame. That was another big thing for me, because the AIS had been such a huge part of my development. The AIS is always going to have a special place in my heart, not only for my years there but also because of their medical team, physios and conditioning coaches who helped me through my numerous injuries, post my time at the institute. It's the home of sport in Australia, the home of basketball, and I have great friendships that were developed there. That induction meant a lot to me.

23

• • •

South Korea

After the Worlds, I had three months off before taking up the contract to play in South Korea, and so I decided to take a vacation in Spain as well as make a quick trip to Russia to visit some friends over there. It was the first time I'd ever done anything like that, travelling without any basketball commitments, and it felt quite liberating. All of my prior travel had involved focusing on playing and training, my only holiday time came when I was home in Australia.

I'd been offered contracts from different parts of the world—Europe, South America, Asia. I could have played anywhere, but I chose South Korea because it was a shorter season and a lot less taxing than the nearly eight months of a European season. I also thought it would be a good stepping stone if I ever wanted to go to Europe for an entire season later on down the track.

I wasn't the only Opal playing overseas in 2007, Belinda and Penny were both playing for different teams in Italy and for Phoenix in the US, Suzy was playing in Russia, Kristi in France, and Tully was playing for Indiana in the US and the Capitals back home. The WNBL in Australia just couldn't match the money paid overseas for top players.

I arrived in Seoul just after Christmas, on 26 December, with Mum and Dad, and it was snowing! I'd certainly travelled to cold countries before, but never lived in one. Coming from an Australian summer, and playing in Seattle in summer, the concept of playing in the cold was completely new to me. We arrived the week before the pre-season training started, and we travelled around Seoul and did a bit of sightseeing in what was to be my new home for four months—it was really icy outside. Mum and Dad stayed for the first three weeks I was there, coming to training, catching buses to games and watching me play. I missed them when they had to leave.

My contract was with the Samsung Bichumi (Samsung Insurance) team, and I was given a three-bedroom apartment in the Samsung employee building to stay in, across the quadrangle from the courts. The other girls in my team, the nationals, lived in a dormitory located near the courts in the same complex, where they ate, slept and relaxed. All my food was paid for, I could go out whenever I wanted—all foreign players were treated like that, not so the nationals, Korean players had a curfew. My teammates were lovely and I did feel bad about how they lived, but I supposed it was a cultural thing, they didn't know any other way of living during a season and didn't seem to worry. But then again, I couldn't understand them even if they did say something, none of them spoke English and I certainly didn't know any Korean. I had an interpreter to help at games, she was a sweet girl and made sure everything I needed was taken care of, but she was a born-again Christian and a lot of what she wanted to talk about centred around her religion, so we didn't have a lot in common.

Each South Korean team was allowed one foreign player, who in most cases was an American. As part of my contract, I had negotiated to have practice only one day a week because of my recurring stress fractures, whereas the rest of the team practised twice a day on non-match days. In the US and Australia, we would only train once a day on days off, I think we're more aware of the effects of overtraining on athletes. Sessions could be weights and individual training, shooting, five on five or cardio work, sprint work and running. I tended to do one on-court session per day and use the other session to light-shoot or lift some weights. We used to run around the outside of the courts for 30 minutes after practice, just for light cardio, and it worked, it was good for my body. I didn't have to go through all the usual pounding, and I became super-fit.

A month after I arrived, I was invited to the Australian Embassy for an Australia Day party, and my interpreter came with me. It was her first experience of 'Aussie culture' and from what I could tell, I think she enjoyed it. There were a lot of Aussies there, mostly businesspeople, and the party itself was pretty amazing. There were some Aussie musicians doing their versions of our favourite barbecue anthems, and of course lots of VB and Jacob's Creek wines, it was great just to hear Aussie accents and speak English again.

My teammates were the sweetest most delightful girls, but it was hard communicating without knowing each other's language. I picked up some of the Korean language, but can't remember any of it now. The language barrier could be interesting at times—one day I decided to impress my teammates by using a word that our coach said all the time, but it turned out to be a swear word that females are not supposed to use, as my somewhat shocked interpreter explained to me afterwards. Our coach was different, I found him over the top by Australian coaching standards. We trained against the under-18 boys' team, so we didn't have to practise against each other and could learn to work together as a team competing with an opposition. One of the boys arrived late one practice and the coach made him kneel beside the court and proceeded to whack him on top of his head with his knuckles. That was his punishment, which I found horrible, but everyone else seemed to just accept it.

It was tough playing against young boys, they were cocky and full of themselves, wanting to make a point. In Seattle, we'd often train against stronger, taller male players, adult men. We'd have some pretty epic battles, and we all became really good friends over time. There were two brothers from South Korea playing in Seattle who I knew well, Dan and Eric, their mother was Korean and their father was American, and they played in the Korean men's league. By this stage, I'd played five years in Seattle and all those who played in the US had become like family. Only Dan was playing in South Korea that season, and he became one of my closest friends during that period. We would meet up and go out after every game—nobody told me not to— often with the other foreigners, just go out and have fun. I was able to connect with people I cared about, and to this day I'm still really good friends with Dan. The professional basketball fraternity is pretty small, and I already knew a lot of the other imports, and it was really good to be able to spend time with them. All of those lovely people are so far away now, but I have memories from those days to last a lifetime. Sometimes I wouldn't get home until the sun was coming up, and the coach would be standing out the front of my building smoking a cigarette, and he'd just shake his head at me. I'm sure he had something to say about it, but I didn't speak the language—ignorance was bliss.

In Seoul, I had the time of my life, other than with the kimchi, I still don't understand why they love to eat that stuff so much. I was happy, had really good friends and I didn't have to fly for games, because it's a small enough country that you can travel by bus to the away games. That was one thing I absolutely loved about that place, I never had to worry about flying in season—at all.

I had a blast playing over there and it began to show, because I started scoring better than I ever had before in my career, I was just on another planet. I played so well because I could focus on my game and my teammates were great fun, I was truly enjoying playing basketball with them. As a team, we didn't start the season off so well, but we improved quickly. Towards the end of the regular season I scored 56 points in one game against the Kumba Redwings, a league record, after scoring 47 points in a game just two weeks before. I took out International MVP of the South Korean league at the end of the season, averaging a huge 29.5 points per game, and was looking forward to another two years of fun playing in South Korea in between my WNBA and Opals commitments.

Nata Hejkova, the coach of Shabtai's new team, Spartak Moscow Region, came to Seoul to visit her nephew and talked me into going back with her to Russia and playing at the end of their season. As soon as I got there, Shabtai was in my ear about leaving Samsung Bichumi and playing for him. American players Diana Taurasi, Sue Bird and Tina Thompson were already playing with his team and I arrived just before the quarterfinals started, after the team had already taken out the EuroLeague Women's title, defeating the Spanish team Ros Casares Valencia only two weeks before.

Our last game before the finals was against Samara—in Samara. A couple of local fans, who were mad that we were winning that game and close to taking the series, covered their faces with balaclavas and scarves and stormed the court during the game. My first instinct was to run out the door, and then I got a little mad myself and, well, let's just say I *didn't* end up running out the door!

In the Russian league finals I averaged 30 minutes a game, and we won through the quarterfinals and semi-finals before winning three of the last five games. Shabtai was delighted.

I was supposed to go back to Korea for two more years in between my WNBA commitments, but Shabtai managed to negotiate my contract out of South Korea. He paid it out and offered me more than I could refuse, and I before I knew it I was contracted to play for him after the 2007 WNBA season.

24

...

Pushing Myself

Arriving back in Seattle for the 2007 season I was physically at my peak. I felt quicker, and more in tune with my body at training, than I had at any time previously in my career, and I'd been injury-free for six months. Four weeks into the season I felt like nothing could stop me. I was always at my happiest when I was playing basketball, and by this time all the youngsters, my age group, were starting to come through the ranks and were becoming better players. It was more fun going to events and games because I was with my peers, rather than being the youngest all the time.

We played a game against Washington on 24 July, our tenth match of the season, and I managed 47 points and set a WNBA league high for a single-game scoring total. That's since been beaten, and we lost that game by one point, so it wasn't such a great performance. I want to say that it felt good at the time, but because our coach was disappointed and really pissed that we'd lost that game, and the rest of the girls were down, there was no room for personal satisfaction.

We made it to the playoffs, but lost two of our three games to Phoenix and didn't progress. I was named defensive player of the year, and a member of the All-WNBA first team, comprising the best five in the league, and became an All-Star for the sixth time. I was also the youngest and fastest player to reach 4000 points in the WNBA that year, which they made a big deal of at Seattle and in the sports media, but I really think I'd become a bit indifferent about it all, a bit blasé about the accolades and associated hype.

All season the media were plugging the possibility of a second MVP in the WNBA as the finals were approaching. When the MVP was announced, I'd received 473 points, with the San Antonio guard Becky Hammon coming second on 254 points. I was completely honoured—to win two MVPs in the WNBA was monumental, an accolade that could not be ignored. As huge as that was, I was just as happy that I was physically fit and had stayed healthy throughout the season. After that horror run with my shin splints, it was good to feel in control of my body again.

The year 2007 was another unbelievable time in my career. The Beijing Olympics were a year away, and I felt I needed to get even stronger to win that Olympic gold— despite all my achievements and awards I still didn't believe

I was good enough. I thought I needed to beef up another 10 kilos, so as I prepared to go back for the long Russian and European season in November I trained even harder, wearing heavy weight belts in an attempt to build myself up even more. Once again, I was pushing my body to its limits. I had to be better.

■   ■   ■

Playing year-round is the nature of basketball at an elite level, athletes' careers are short and we need to earn as much as we can before we retire. Being in Russia meant we were having to fly all the time to away games, across the country and then into Europe. By this stage, Aeroflot was replacing its fleet with new jets, unlike the horrid planes I'd experienced before in Russia, and Shabtai had us on private jets most of the time, when commercial flights didn't fit in with the game schedules. But there were still problems to compound my apprehension about flying.

It was common for us to get to the airport at six in the morning to catch a flight, and more often than not the other passengers would be having vodka shots instead of coffee for breakfast—happily getting drunk first thing in the morning, but that's Russia. Those same passengers would have more vodka shots on the plane, and under the influence they would become loud, red-faced and sweaty (when the outside temperature was something like minus 20 degrees Celsius outside). I didn't understand the language, so I had no idea what those drunk men on board my plane were yelling about, and it all felt rather strange to me. It was a totally different experience, so bizarre and funny to look back on now, but it didn't seem funny to me at the time.

I remember one time when we were playing in the north of Russia, we flew there on a rickety old charter plane—not one of the private jets with big comfortable leather seats that Shabtai would usually organise—it was travelling dodge. We finished the game and went to the airport and were told 'You can't fly tonight, sorry', and I was worried that there must have been something wrong with the plane, but it turned out the pilot was drunk. We had to get on a really old train and travel nearly 24 hours back, but if we had time between games and training I still preferred travelling by train to flying.

I have so many flying stories from Russia about trips that made me uneasy. But there were other aspects of being there that certainly didn't help. On one occasion we were supposed to be flying from Ekaterinburg back to Moscow with Aeroflot, but the game went late, into overtime. Commercial airlines have to depart on time, they always have a strict schedule and don't wait for anyone, but this plane actually waited for us. Shabtai had made a phone call from the stadium, I was there when he did that, and the airline delayed the flight for us, all the people booked on the plane had to hang around for an extra hour at the airport.

It would be like someone calling Qantas and asking them to hold a flight for an hour—don't worry about the people on the plane, or the airline schedule. It was unbelievable, but that's the sort of person Shabtai was, the man had power.

He loved being around the girls, the team. His third wife Anna was lovely, she was one of my teammates in Spartak Moscow. She'd been captain of the national team in Athens when Russia won bronze, but she'd retired from the role by this time. Shabtai and Anna had young twin boys, and he had two beautiful daughters from his previous marriages.

Shabtai could certainly be charming. Shabs, we called him, or Poppa. He wanted me to call him Poppa, he treated me like he would have treated his daughter, but I wasn't. There was always that level of expectation because I was paid, all of us were paid well to play, we were his. There were other foreigners in the same boat as me, because probably the three best players in the world—Sue, Diana and myself—were playing for Spartak Moscow at the time. For some reason, not long after I arrived, our team name changed to Sparta & K, apparently Shabtai had had a falling out with the Spartak club, so created his own name for his team. Making his own rules, that was so typical of him. It's what Shabtai did—made his own rules in life.

He had obscene wealth, and close connections with all sorts of businessmen. I'd never been exposed to anything like that before. He rented out a big house for Sue, Diana and myself with a pool, spa and sauna, whatever we wanted he would provide us with, to make things as homely as possible.

The apartment was actually half of a large house, and there was a family living in the other half. Their babushka (grandmother) would come in and clean the house for us every day when we were at practice, do our washing, laundry, everything, she was a lovely old woman but didn't speak a lick of English.

Shabtai would take us to the most remarkable restaurants and we'd have the best food. I love borscht, beetroot soup, so he would make a point of taking me to places that served good borscht. He'd give us money or his credit card to go shopping, took us out to nightclubs, gave us holidays—we had a house, a driver, got whatever we wanted whenever we wanted. He once organised box seats at a Marilyn Manson concert in Russia for me, because he knew I loved his music. It was an eye-opening experience, I'd never seen so much wealth splashed around.

One time we had to go to Paris to play for a week, and Shabtai suggested we leave a couple of days early and do some shopping. After our last game in Russia before the Paris trip I saw him hand this wad of cash, 10 000 Euros, to one of the other girls for us to use as spending money in France. I saw her put the money in her bag, and that evening we went to a nightclub and the money was taken, the bag was still there, but the money was gone. Someone with the team must have known about the money, someone saw it. If I'd had that much money in a bag I wouldn't have put it down anywhere. I can't remember if we ever told Shabs, I'm sure we did, but there was no fuss made about it.

Another memorable time, Shabtai hosted a major European All-Star game against a team of the best foreigners, American and Australian, and he flew in the American rapper Kelis to perform at the match after-party. She came back and partied until late with us at our house, with everybody else who was there, a lot of Americans, the players from the European league. That night was indicative of my time in Russia, it was just unbelievable really. Shabtai wanted it to be a good experience for us, he would have done anything for us, he genuinely cared for us as people, not just as basketballers.

Shabs did want us to be happy, but once we were under contract there was a shift in how he saw and treated us. He wouldn't deal with my agent, he didn't want to pay their fee, he basically felt like his relationship with us would trump everything. So, after the first contract, there was no further negotiation about what he came to us with—but the money was so good I didn't question it. I think I went through a couple of agents when I was in Russia, but that was where the big money was being made and Shabtai wouldn't work with them, so I let them go. That's just the way it was, like I said, the money was so good who was I to argue with him? I'd try to, but there was no point, because he would always win. He made me feel as though I had to trust him even though there was this underlying cynicism and worry. It was the strangest feeling.

Sue was one of my best friends, still is, both she and Diana were my age, we were able to go out and do stuff together, and our half of the house had plenty of bedrooms, six bedrooms and an attic, a heap of bathrooms, three or four of them. It was easy living with those two girls, but even though we had each other, it could still be lonely.

In fact, Russia became the coldest, loneliest place in the world for me. All that dark history seemed to weigh me down. The culmination of everything that was happening to me in Russia, the flying, feeling owned, meant I started to fall to pieces, all I wanted to do when not playing was go to bed. It was the middle of the Russian winter, the sun wasn't up when we went to practice, we'd train for two hours, go outside and it would finally be light at eleven or twelve o'clock, then we'd go back home, sleep, get up, eat, go to practice and come back out and it was dark again, go home, go to bed. After games, we might go out and have a drink, but I didn't really reflect on how I was feeling, I just had to keep going. That was the head space I was in. I don't think the other girls in Russia felt so down, and if they did, it was never talked about.

When I was younger I didn't stop to think about the times when I felt low, I just sort of dealt with it, no matter what I was doing I still had to get up and go to practice, play basketball. And now it was happening again. Perhaps Sue knew I wasn't happy, but we never talked about it. Shabtai knew, we did talk, and he tried to support me. He really did care, he knew I was struggling. Playing basketball was what ultimately got me through that period.

We made the EuroLeague finals in April 2008. We'd played the semi-final against Ekaterinburg two days before the final, and early in the game it felt like the fat pad under-neath the ball of my foot was blistering. At half-time, I took my sock off, put Vaseline on my foot and covered it again before going back on court. It was a big game that we needed to win to progress to the finals, and I was playing well—but towards the end of the match, as I changed direction I felt the ball of my foot rip, and immediately called for a time out. My coach and teammates were asking what was wrong and I couldn't answer. I sat down and took my shoe and sock off, and blood just went everywhere. I'd managed to sheer three layers off the ball of my left foot when I'd turned on it. I was subbed off, and we won the game 78–68, but the final against BK Brno in the Czech Republic was just two days later. I wanted to play, to win for the team, for the girls, for Shabtai, so I had salt baths every three to four hours to try and dry out the freshly exposed skin, one of the most painful experiences I've ever had to endure. Mandy Berntsen, my Australian physio, had been flown over to Russia and was working with Shabtai's team as the physiotherapist, because she was the best in the world, and Shabtai only paid for the best. Mandy got me through that injury. She rang the Opals doctor, who told her over the phone how to bandage my foot so I could play. We won the EuroLeague title for a second time and I was named MVP of the EuroLeague Final Four that year, but it was one of the most painful injuries I'd ever pushed myself to play through. We went back to Russia and also won the Russian league, then it was straight back to the WNBA, and preparing for Beijing.

25

...

On to Beijing

Arriving for the 2008 WNBA season I met the Storm's new head coach, Brian Agler, who'd been appointed after Anne resigned. Brian had been the assistant coach with Phoenix and the San Antonio Silver Stars, and was a totally different kind of coach—like Anne and Tom he was flexible and able to identify what would bring out the best in his players, but unlike Anne he showed little emotion.

I loved the way Brian coached, in fact if I was ever to be a coach I would want to be like him, because he understood his players both individually and collectively. He really got the best out of his girls, he had good professional relationships with each and every one of us, knowing we were all different. Sometimes coaches are so stuck in their ways, in their own mind, they're not willing to bring in ideas gleaned from other coaches and other teams. If I see a team that's really successful, I personally always want to dissect the parts that really appeal to me and try to incorporate that into what I do. I think that would be my biggest thing with coaches, being flexible with their players and their offensive plays, and being able to work around individual players. Coaches who are flexible are the best.

I didn't play the last four WNBA games prior to the Olympic break, as I left the US to train with the Opals. Harley had retired from basketball and I'd been named captain, and I needed to rejoin my team. The lead-up games to that Olympics are all a bit of a blur for me, mentally I really wasn't there, but I was certainly able to compete, playing some of my best basketball.

I was selected for the Opals without having to try out, that's one pressure I didn't have to deal with most of my career. The only time I really ever had to compete to make the Opals squad was before the 1998 world championship, but once I was in, I was in. I didn't play many games for Australia after I made the WNBA, only the major tournaments—by contrast, in the lead-up to the Games, most of the 2008 Opals team had been together and training at home. They'd also travelled to Europe to play, and competed in a couple of week-long tournaments in Asia. There would have been plenty of time together and plenty of training.

After I arrived back in Australia from the US, we hosted and played against Brazil—who were fourth in the world—and won both games in Wollongong and Sydney, before heading to China for the prestigious FIBA Diamond Ball for women. We won against the host nation China 84–79, and then Mali the next day by 112–43, before playing the US in the final.

As expected, it was a tough, close game. The US were ahead one point at the end of the first quarter and then pulled ahead to be six points in front at half-time. We each scored 21 points in the third quarter, and in the fourth managed 17 points to their 15. It wasn't enough, with the final score US 71, Australia 67.

The Opals were ranked number two in the world behind the US. Our team was a great mix of experience and talent, I was playing some of my best basketball, I knew personally that I wouldn't be satisfied with anything but gold at the Olympics. That was my focus, that's what kept me going.

My right ankle was playing up again and I had to manage it carefully. There was no way I wasn't going to play. I wanted to play, and headed with my team to Beijing.

We won the opening game at the 2008 Olympic Games with an 83–64 victory over Belarus. An 80–65 victory over Brazil was next, followed by a 90–62 win over Korea, before meeting Russia, placed third in the world, who we comfortably defeated 75–55. The Opals once again were going into an Olympic quarterfinal unbeaten. We defeated the Czech Republic 79–46, then China in the semi-final 90–56, to book a place in the gold medal match against the US.

There's no easy way to say this. We lost by 27 points, and it was devastating. The US had us from the start, and when the game ended I think we were all in tears. We had silver, but we had so wanted that gold. To rub salt into our wounds, Lisa Leslie wore her previous three Olympic gold medals on to the dais where she was to receive her fourth with the team. It was incredible to think she'd brought them all with her. Apparently, an official saw her wearing them as her team came out, and told her to put them under her jacket, but she took them out again as the American national anthem played. As much as it was so not something I would do, I wouldn't know what it was like to have an Olympic gold medal—so I'm not sure how I would act with one, let alone four, around my neck.

After the medal ceremony, I went over and gave my parents a huge hug, and handed my silver medal to Mum, but was too upset to attend the post-match media conference with our coach Jan. We'd convinced ourselves we could win, would win, but it was not to be, and we were all truly devastated. I was shattered.

■　■　■

Before the closing ceremony we'd had a few drinks, someone had managed to get alcohol into the village, it just landed in my hand and I was feeling the effects of it by the time we marched in. As the nations milled around in the middle of the arena, I went up and gave the Chinese basketballer Yao Ming, who seems to tower above everyone at 2.34 metres (7 feet 8 inches), a big hug. Someone snapped the photo. I knew him, I'd met him before, and full of liquid courage I went and gave him a hug—and all of a sudden it was all over social media, with stories insinuating that I was having some sort of affair with him. The basketball fraternity is really small, we all know each other, it could have been anyone I hugged. There were thousands of athletes at the closing ceremony. He was just there, and I didn't think.

Being good at sport, I know you become public property, but the reaction to that whole incident was ludicrous to me, it still is. I was surprised when my teammates were talking about it the next day, I was wondering how the hell they knew, given I'd pretty much forgotten about it already. I only saw the newspaper reports a day or so later, I don't think I was even on social media back then. So that's how I found out how huge the story actually was, when people who didn't usually comment started saying stuff to me, my friends, my family, people in America. I went right into my shell, I didn't speak to anybody, I felt sick. I completely shut down.

26

. . .

Getting Help

I may as well have scrubbed the period immediately following that Olympics out of my life, erased it, because I was
gone. Although I didn't think I was playing that well, my
stats were good. But as for me, as a person, I was miserable.
I wasn't in a good place mentally.

My ankle had continued to deteriorate playing through
the Beijing Olympics, and it was decided that I needed
surgery, so I headed back home to Australia rather than
return to Seattle. I had to miss the rest of the WNBA season,
which I was also feeling really down about. Mum and Dad
picked me up from the airport, and the emotions associated with coming down from the Olympics really hit me,
I couldn't speak, even to my own parents. It was so hard on

them. They are and always have been there for me and done everything they could for me, but I was that far gone that I wasn't able to communicate, even with them. When I did eventually speak, I was feeling so hurt that I think it came across as anger.

I had my ankle surgery and rehabilitated for a couple of weeks in the small, dark apartment I owned at the time in Sydney—it suited my mental state in a way, dark and closed in. I was only in Sydney for a couple of weeks after surgery, and then I went back to the US to be with and support Seattle, even though I couldn't play, while they finished the WNBA season. They were defeated by the LA Sparks two games to one in the playoffs. The 2008 WNBA season was over.

I came back to Australia. They talk about the 'black dog' of depression, well that was it, that's where I was, and it was the darkest most horrible place to be. The minute I opened my mouth all that came out was anger and bitterness. I had no clue how Mum and Dad could stand to be around me, and I think I may have even vocalised that, but they were there, as always. They helped me, stayed with me and persisted with me. There was a point where I wasn't getting out of bed until about four o'clock in the afternoon, it took me a good week or two to get just to that stage, and Mum would give me a glass of wine and all this emotion would come out. I was struggling.

I eventually went on to antidepressants, I needed to. Facing that realisation was hard for me, I guess it was an admission of weakness. I didn't want to tell my family, but it was evident to Mum and Dad that I was in trouble, I'd really shut down, I was a mess. It wasn't something that was done to me, it was something that eventuated—take the environment that I'd been in, then add the elite athlete side of it, add that I'm a woman, and that I stand out in the community in more ways than one, add that I felt owned, I *was* owned, I was not my own person. All of this compounded by losing another Olympic gold medal match, having another possible career-ending injury and needing yet more surgery. I was struggling with everything. I felt physically ill all the time, I'd lost so much weight. Going back and looking at photos I was rake thin and back to my 2000 weight, which was before I'd actually physically developed. I was sick, sick as a dog.

While I was in Russia, I hadn't had time to sort out my mental state and speak to a psychologist as I'd descended into depression. I'd spoken to a sports psychologist at the AIS when I was back in Australia just before the Beijing Olympics, but it was only a short amount of time before I was off again travelling, playing and preparing for the Games. I couldn't maintain that relationship with the psychologist, being so-time poor, and having a one-off appointment didn't really work. However, in our conversation he did suggest that I go on antidepressants, that they would help even me out—I'd declined at the time, but now I was back in Australia I realised I needed help. I went to my team doctors, talked to them and got a prescription, but apart from them I didn't tell anyone, Mum and Dad didn't even know. When they did realise I was taking them we still didn't talk about it. I think the only person I really ever spoke to about this was Katrina Hibbert. We were sitting beside the lake in Albury, I remember talking to her about returning to Russia, and feeling a hell of a lot better being out in the warm sun rather than being back there in their bleak winter. It felt good to talk about it—but a couple of weeks later I was heading back to cold, dark Russia.

27

...

Back to Russia

My behaviour had been up and down throughout my twenties, even before I went to play for Shabtai, and I think I could quite easily have taken that route into depression much earlier. When I'd started going through all my mental health issues in Russia, I'd just wanted to be home in Australia—I knew I could help myself by removing myself from the situation, but I also wanted to play basketball for a living. I loved playing, those two hours on court were the best part of my day, but I wanted to earn the big money. I couldn't make a living like that from basketball back in Australia.

We were playing nearly every weekend in the Russian league, as well as competing in a different country every week as part of the European league. We were flying all over Europe, and given the mental state I was in, my anxiety about planes was worse than ever. I just took more medication. I don't know if it was helping me as it should have, but I managed to get to games and play. My teammates didn't know, I didn't talk about it, so I isolated myself even more. I drank a lot, too, I probably shouldn't have been drinking as much as I was. We'd play, we'd go out, I drank, it all got too much for me.

Mum and I were talking only a couple of years ago about some players constantly bitching and complaining about things, and she said, 'I don't know if you remember, but when you were in Russia, you were on the phone upset about things every day', and I don't even recall that. I was so miserable, and I just couldn't get out of it. It got to the stage that whenever I had free time I went to bed. I stopped going out with the girls and just stayed home. Shabtai wanted us to have fun and enjoy our time there, but I didn't anymore, the shine had gone.

I knew Shabtai had enrolled me in university in Moscow, but I never attended. I'm not sure what I was supposed to have studied, but I went into Shabtai's office one day and he surprised me by handing over an official-looking certificate written in Russian and said, 'Congratulations, you've finished a year of university'. I was like, 'What?'. I didn't do a day of study, I don't think I would have been up to it anyway.

It was a different kind of time for me. I was blinded by everything Shabtai gave me, which included diamonds when

we won tournaments. He treated his imports really well—
but in our team there were young Russian women from all
over the country playing basketball for Shabtai, and I don't
think they were looked after the same way we were. Women
were treated differently in that part of the world, in all of
eastern Europe. I wasn't really thinking about it at the time,
I was seeing it but not acknowledging it. I was just playing
and getting through each day.

I hadn't really seen or caught up with Paulie—who'd
always been my compass for dealing with issues—since I'd
gone to Russia and America. During that time I'd grown up,
and everything she'd taught me about equality and power
play had gone by the wayside, I didn't really think about it,
I just played basketball, it was my heyday. I'd been partying
a lot, especially in America and South Korea, socialising
with my teammates. I wasn't in the nest anymore, I was
out in the world, just being young and not overly analyti-
cal about anything. When I went to Russia and things got
out of control, a lot of these issues around power started
coming back up for me—but as for acknowledging it and
trying to understand it, that didn't quite happen. Shabtai
was a dominant male, I felt a complete loss of control, but I
didn't want to think about it.

Shabtai decided to send me on a holiday to Israel with
another one of my teammates as a congratulation for
winning an important game. He'd taken us on little holidays
and trips and adventures before. Sue and Diana had gone
to Israel previously with Shabtai, and they'd told me about

When Mum was in her early twenties and playing overseas representing Australia.

Mum was one of the youngsters on the Australian team before she earned her number 15.

My father in his early twenties showing his athleticism in a club match.

Jumping Jack can't beat his 'Jill'

Sydney basket-baller Gary "Jumping" Jackson, has decided that he must lift his game.

By GRAHAM BURKE

GARY JACKSON pivots on his left foot to put himself in a scoring position during one-on-one practice at Albert Park.

After all, what male likes to be beaten by a female?

Jackson, who is training with Lindsay Gaze's Australian squad at Albert Park for the Oceania Olympic eliminations and the U.S.-China-Hongkong tour, recently became engaged to Albury basketballer, Maree Bennie.

Jackson's ego is in pieces. He has had several one-on-one contests with his fiancee, but never beaten her.

One-on-one is a basketball duel where one player pits his skills against the other.

Jackson admitted today that it was "a little embarrassing" to think that a girl could beat him at basketball.

"Maree is no ordinary girl," he said.

Jackson is right there. Maree was Australia's best player at the recent world championships in Columbia.

They make a tall couple. Jackson is 195cm (6ft 5in) tall and Maree is 190cm (6ft 3in).

They met at an after-match party during last year's Australian championships in Sydney and announced their engagement after Maree returned from overseas a fortnight ago.

Jackson, a sales representative, said they hoped to be married towards the end of next year and make their home at Albury.

He plays basketball for City of Sydney, Sydney's second-ranked team.

This is the first time he has been chosen in an Australian squad, but it will be his second trip to the U.S.

Jackson toured the West Coast with the NSW State team in 1973.

The Australian team will leave from Sydney on November 15.

Their U.S. itinerary will cover the eight universities in the Pacific Athletic Conference and also Brigham Young University.

The Australians' first game will be against Washington in Seattle on November 18.

The team will then move on to play Washington State in Pullman on November 19, California at Berkeley on November 20, UCLA at Los Angeles on November 21, Southern California in Los Angeles on November 22, Oregon in Eugene on November 24, Oregon State at Portland on November 25, and Stanford in Stanford, California, on November 26.

The BYU game will be in Provo, Utah, on November 29.

Games in China and Hongkong will follow.

Jackson's chances of representing Australia at next year's Montreal Olympics will depend on his performances during the tour.

Match made in basketball heaven!!! Dad's still just as proud of Mum today.

Mum with Dad's mum and dad. Dad is at the back with his brother Neil and sister-in-law Edith.

With Dad.

Mum, Dad, Ross and me in my grandmother's living room in Albury.

Mum with her parents.

With Ross in front of our house at Endeavour Hills. I'm wearing Mum's national team tracksuit that Nan cut down for me. I would have been aged eight.

At the under-12s state championships representing the Albury Cougars. We were playing Newcastle.

Here we are as the under-12 state champions.

JAN 1994

IT HAS ALWAYS BEEN AN ATHLETES DREAM TO BE IN THE OLYMPICS AND
NOW ITS MYN EXCEPT THIS ONE IS DIFFERENT, IT WILL BE THE YEAR
2000 OLYMPICS AND I WILL DO EVERYTHING TO GET IN IT. THE YEAR
2000 OLYMPICS IS 6YEARS AWAY AND I HAVE 6 YEARS TO SHOW EVERYONE
WHAT I AM MADE OF I AM NOT A BAG OF WOSS LIKE EVERYONE CALL ME.
I WILL BE 19 IN THE YEAR 2000 AND WILL BE PREPARED FOR ALL THE
CHALLENGERS I WILL FACE. I WILL PLAY MY HARDEST FROM THIS DAY ON
WITH DETERMINATION AND SKILL. I FIGHT TILL THE END AND WHATEVER
DARES TO COME AGAINST ME SHALL NOT SUCCED BUT WISH TO GOD IT
NEVER DOES IT AGAIN. I AM THE BEST AND ALWAYS WILL BE NOTHING
CAN STOP ME NOW.

LAUREN JACKSON

My mission statement written when I was twelve.

One of the earliest battles against Lisa
Leslie in the lead up to 2000 Olympics.
(GETTY IMAGES/HAMISH BLAIR)

When we won WNBA Championship in
2004.

Sports Illustrated Swimsuit Edition.

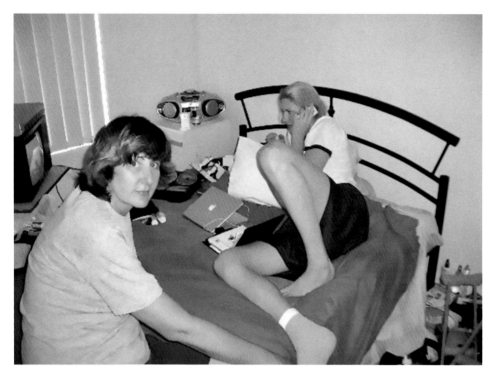

Post ankle surgery, recovering at home with my parents in 2004.

The first game I played with the Albury Wodonga Lady Bandits, the day after Commonwealth Games finished in 2006.

Seattle fan's support in the 2007 WNBA season for most valued player of the league. (TERRENCE VACCARO/NBAE/GETTY IMAGES)

On the World Championship gold medal podium, standing with some of my dearest friends. (GETTY IMAGES/JOE MURPHY)

Anne Donovan coaching me 2007. (TERRENCE VACCARO/NBAE/GETTY IMAGES)

I was named most valued player in
WNBA 2007.

Messing around with Sue in 2010 on the bench during one of the games.

Sue, Shabtai, Diana and me during a magazine photo shoot. (BOB MARTIN/SPORTS ILLUSTRATED/GETTY IMAGES)

As flag bearer in the 2012 London Olympics opening ceremony. (CAMERON SPENCER/ GETTY IMAGES)

With the World Championship trophy.

A Chinese healing remedy I was given to try and mend my knee. I have no idea what it was, but it didn't work very well.

China early 2014. Doing a little shopping, Mum and I stumbled across this lovely bride in a pretty dress atop toilet paper.

New Year's Eve 2013/2014. Dinner after a win, everyone was pretty happy!

With the beautiful bride-to-be! Suzy Batkovic one of my dearest friends. No one can make me laugh like this woman!

With Mum and Prime Minister Julia Gillard at the Lodge on Australia Day 2012.

Jersey Retirement, Seattle Storm 2015. (JOSHUA HUSTON/NBAE/GETTY IMAGES)

With Sue at my Jersey Retirement, Seattle Storm, 2015.

The Lauren Jackson Sport Centre, where I grew up playing, in 2011.

Under 'Lauren Jackson Walk', the day I retired from the National team at the AIS in 2015.

At the Lauren Jackson
Sport Centre opening
showing young players
memorabilia.

With Mum, Dad and
Ross at the Lauren
Jackson Sport Centre
opening.

My brother Ross and sister-in-law
Nicole.

With Governor-General Sir Peter Cosgrove, his wife 'Auntie' Lynne and Mum and Dad after receiving my Order of Australia in 2015.

My niece Laura and nephew Fletcher and my beautiful little boy Harry, who's first Christmas was hard because Santa scared him . . . a lot!!!

being with him there, how they would walk with him down the street and how well known he was. Some people hated him, some loved him, but I didn't know what that was about.

He sent us to Tel Aviv, a beautiful sunny city, where both his daughters live, he had a lot of family there. Shabtai organised a car and driver for us so we could visit the other special places that Israel is renowned for. We were in the country for three days or so, and it ended up being a pretty full-on experience.

In Jerusalem, we took a couple of tours, did the walk taken by Jesus with his cross before his crucifixion, saw the place where it's claimed he was resurrected, visited churches, did our best to see everything. Our driver took us up to the mountain overlooking Jerusalem as part of a day trip, and as we drove past a university there were dumpsters on the road on fire, and kids started throwing rocks at our car. I'd never had that feeling of being in a danger zone before, and to compound things, on the way back to Tel Aviv we had a small car accident. I was on so much medication at that point that I just wasn't myself—sleeping pills, anti-depressants, Valium, were all numbing my feelings. But even though I was heavily medicated, I was still aware of being in a hostile environment.

Travel is supposed to open up your mind, but I think the history of the countries I'd experienced from my travels playing basketball had added a weight on my shoulders that I'd never felt in Australia. I was born and raised here, and am comfortable here, but eastern Europe, Israel, Lithuania,

Germany, all those countries with so much history that we've read about and studied in school, they felt melancholy to me. I should be so thankful that I had the opportunity to go there and experience all those things that I would otherwise never have seen, but I was definitely affected by the weight of past events that were so beyond my comprehension at the time. The other thing was that I had been playing in Europe and Asia in winter, the trees had no leaves on them, everything was literally grey and gloomy—and that was exactly how I felt, too, I couldn't lift myself out of it.

That season there was also something going on with Shabtai that I couldn't quite put my finger on, he just started talking differently to us. His father had died in Israel and he went over for the funeral, and when he returned he told us he had bought the burial plot next to his dad's. I thought that was fair enough, but he was saying stuff that made me think things weren't quite right.

Towards the end of that second season, something happened that made me even more uneasy. Following a match, our driver took Sue, Diana and myself to a shopping mall where the three of us often used to go and have a meal after games, we had our favourite spots. Our driver thought there was a car behind us that was following us. As there'd been a fan infatuated with Diana at the time, we were wary. When we got to the shopping mall we noticed this guy dressed all in black following us everywhere, and it was really unnerving. We decided to walk around the shops, and whenever we looked back he'd always be there. We went to dinner, and he was wandering around out the front of the restaurant, so we called Shabtai and he said, 'Don't worry, he's security'. That shocked us, and we were all thinking 'Why do we need security?'. It was just one of those moments where things felt really bizarre—he'd organised for us to have security and wouldn't explain why. What the hell was going on? You don't put security on people for no reason. There were a few times like that, and it took a further toll on my mental state. We might not have been in immediate danger, but that season it felt like there was something else going on. I certainly wasn't flourishing as a human being, I don't think I was a good person to be around at all.

I came back to Australia and was contracted to go back to Russia for the following season. It had reached the point where I felt really controlled and powerless. Shabtai still wouldn't deal with my agents, I couldn't play anywhere else, he was paying me so much money that it was almost impossible to take up other options. Money is such a compelling factor when you're playing a professional sport, especially being a woman, as we're often paid much less than men. I was there for the money, even though I was uncomfortable, and I had a fairly serious internal battle going on.

28

...

Back

In Russia, I'd been using a weight jacket during my individual training sessions, trying to bulk up because I'd lost so much weight. I was down to about 70 something kilos, which was very light for a 1.96 metre athlete. It made me faster, but not stronger. While I was training with the weightbelt, doing sprints to build up muscle, my back had started to get achy. But as usual, I'd just taken medication and played on.

I came back to Australia and was a bridesmaid at Suzy Batkovic's wedding, which I know was lovely, but I remember so little, everything at that time was a bit of a blur. I was back in Australia for a month and that really helped, being home and resting, before heading back to Seattle.

My 2009 season with Seattle started well, but I strained my Achilles tendon halfway through and had to rest it for a couple of games. Towards the end of the season there was plenty of media hype about the fact that I was close to scoring 5000 career points, a milestone only reached at that stage by three WNBA players—Lisa Leslie, Tina Thompson and Katie Smith. I achieved it in a game against Atlanta. Later in that same game, there was a free throw awarded to the other team and I went to the free-throw line and lined up. One of the Atlanta players, I can't remember who, shot the free throw and I jumped up to get the rebound and when I landed my back crunched, but I kept playing even though it hurt. The game ended, we lost the game by nine points and the team went into the locker room. I sat down and Brian was having a go at us, saying whatever he was saying, and I shifted forward on the bench and let out the biggest 'FUCK!'. The pain was so excruciating, my body had cooled down and the injury in my back grabbed me as I moved. I remember everyone looking at me and my face going bright red, but nobody said anything, and Brian continued on with his rant. I went to the training room to get my back looked at and was told it was probably just a sprain, and so I played on, for another four games.

That injury happened while we were on the road. We played against Detroit, Indiana and Washington, but in the next game, against Connecticut, I was in so much pain that I collapsed in the locker room post-game. I think it was a mix of pain and frustration at the situation I was in. When I got to my apartment that night I called Scotty Burne, who had been the Opals's team doctor at the 2006 Commonwealth Games and who I trust to this day, and talked to him about my injury and the pain I was experiencing, and he told me to go and get bone scans straight away. So I went the next day, with my coach Brian, who was also really concerned and supportive. I'd been a bit mad at him pushing me to play, but he'd tried to protect me, limiting my time on court while I was injured when everyone thought it was just a bad sprain. We went back to the specialist and were told that I had in fact fractured my back. I'd been playing with two stress fractures in my lumbar spine, one on the left side and one on the right side of my L5 (the fifth lumbar vertebra). The right-hand side was completely fractured, the other was more like a stress fracture.

I was furious that I'd been playing, because I'd probably made the fractures worse. I don't know how I'd even managed to continue in that condition. I'd played through a lot of pain before, and I knew my body well enough to recognise when I'd hurt myself. So when I'd said there was something wrong, I would have hoped to be listened to, especially given that I was a veteran of the game—at this point I was 28 years old. I just felt like I was stuck, and there was nowhere to turn. As it turned out, this was a real turning point for me, it was a lesson. I was the only one who really knew what my body was telling me, and I felt as though I couldn't trust anyone else to make the call.

Everyone in Australia was worried about me, I was a big part of the national team. I was committed to play in Russia, and I had other commitments to other teams. One of the hardest things about playing year-round was that I didn't only have to worry about the team I was currently on if I got injured—I was playing for two or three teams each year, and I had to worry about each of them. An injury would impact all of my contracts, all my commitments, so I was always trying to weigh up what was right for my body as well as whoever I was playing for.

I came straight home to Australia and then had to stay off my feet and not load my back for the next three months, before gradually starting my rehab—which I did at the AIS. I would be heading off to Russia again for another season, but I had to get my back right before I returned. I had to try and get it stronger, I needed to take that amount of time off to let it heal—I couldn't run, there was absolutely no weight-bearing, but in the end my trainer at the AIS, Ross Smith, rehabbed me and got me ready for Russia.

My family were also really concerned about me, they could see I wasn't happy. I was sitting at my uncle Lyle's place and I remember him asking me, 'How are we going to stop you going back to Russia, how do we get you out of that situation?'. I told him half-seriously and half in jest that the only way would be if Shabtai had a heart attack, because I knew he'd already had a triple bypass, either that or he'd have to be murdered. I truly believed it would take one of those two things for me to be released, I felt like he had so much control over me. I believed I could only play in Europe under him, it might have all been in my head, but I know what I saw and I know how I felt and I know what Shabtai said to me as well, 'When you're over here, you play for me'. It was just known, I couldn't play anywhere else in Europe. I once saw him go up and say something to a man on the corner of the basketball court in the Czech Republic, and the guy wet himself. You know when you see something you don't understand or it doesn't quite register and you do a double-take? That's what it was like. It was unbelievable. There were so many times with Shabs that I felt I did that.

Nothing comes for free in life. Shabs knew I was struggling emotionally and he tried to make it better for me, but ultimately I think he put more pressure on me by doing that, and it made me even worse.

Being back in Canberra I reconnected with Paulie and talked to her about what I'd been through. I remember sitting on her loungeroom floor in front of the fire and just breaking down into tears, and she listened and supported me, as she does. In eastern Europe, I'd seen the way women were treated, it's not so much the inequality, it's just that men really have the power over there, the more money you have, the more you get, anything you want, it's yours. Even thinking about Shabtai, he wanted me to play on his team, he got me, that's how it was. In Australia, there's still some talk about women not being equal to men, particularly in sports, because we aren't as strong or as athletic or as big, but it's more covert here than in Russia, where it seemed more overt. I don't know how it is now, but it was a different world when I was there.

BACK

I was staying at Paulie's place because I'd long since sold my house, and I was only training a couple of days a week with Ross at the AIS, and then training back at Albury the other days. Paulie always has a room for me. One night she was away, and there was a massive thunderstorm, it felt like it was straight out of a horror movie. At night, I tend to have my phone on silent, but at about 11 pm I could hear it vibrating. I decided to ignore it. I thought someone was being terribly rude calling me at that hour, and I tried to go back to sleep through the tumultuous thunder and lightning. Eventually I looked at my phone and saw it was Sue. She'd been calling me constantly. I answered and she said, 'Dude, where have you been? Shabtai's dead, he's been murdered'. I was stunned. I didn't sleep the rest of that night and by eight in the morning I was on a plane to Israel for his funeral. It was the most bizarre shit I've ever been through in my life, between the crazy storm and then the news that Shabtai had been killed.

I flew out on Melbourne Cup day, 3 November 2009. The horse that won the cup that year was Shocking, with Crime Scene coming in second.

■　■　■

According to the newspapers, Shabtai von Kalmanovich had been a KGB spy, successful businessman, concert promoter and basketball sponsor. On 2 November 2009, he was shot ten times by an unknown gunman as he sat in his black Mercedes at traffic lights in Moscow waiting for the signal to change. He'd actually been on his way to his office to pick up one of my teammates to take her to a concert, she was lucky she wasn't in his car with him. Nobody knows who shot him, no one was ever arrested.

Shabtai was very important to me. I'm still trying to work out in what way, because there was part of me that loved him and part of me that was so intimidated by him. Shabtai was a scary man, but he was always good to me, he always wanted to try and make me comfortable and happy— I truly believe, though, that our cultures were so different he could never have known what I needed over there. He was involved in a lot of different things, I heard so many stories over the years, and it was hard to decipher what was fact and what was fiction. I know that whatever I heard come out of his mouth was generally true, which is frightening in itself. Looking back, I wish I'd been more present mentally during that time, so I could have asked him more questions and learnt as much as possible from him. The man knew five different languages (at least), he was incredibly intelligent, his life was straight out of a movie. As much as I felt constricted in his world, he really tried to make that time as good as he could for me, for all of us. Some of his later ventures in particular were very honourable, he was extremely generous and he tried to help people, he really did, there was a very kind side to him. The other side, what little I saw, I will never talk about because of his wife Anna and his gorgeous kids, who I still think about to this day, particularly his youngest daughter, who I have seen turn into her own beautiful person.

I still see Shabtai in my dreams, both good and bad dreams.

29

...

Empower Her

Shabtai had a traditional Jewish funeral in Israel. His body was wrapped in a sheet and laid in a synagogue with all the mourners standing around his body for the service. His body was then taken to the grave plot he had bought next to his father's less than a year before. I was standing with my teammates beside the grave, and as they lowered his body into the hole, the sheet fell away and you could see where he'd been shot in the chest. I was right there, but I don't remember exactly what it looked like, it was all a blur, I had to be told about it afterwards. Sue and the rest of my Russian teammates were there, his whole family were there. Anna and all his children, you'd never wish that upon anybody.

After Shabtai's funeral, I arrived back home and went and had a coffee with Graffy. She asked if I wanted to go back to Russia and I simply stated, 'No, I don't'. With Shabtai gone, I knew there would be financial pressure on his team. I also wanted to stay home and take a few weeks off to rehab my back properly so I could make the next WNBA season, which would begin in May, six months away. The WNBL season was about to start, and I knew I much preferred to play for the Capitals again rather than return to Russia. I still had one year of the contract to play in Russia, but because of my back I stayed in Australia. I think this was a welcome relief for the team—money wouldn't be as easy for them to come by when Shabtai wasn't at the helm, and I would have been close to three months late coming back to them by the time my back was fully healed.

Graffy managed to put together a good contract for that season and then a three-year playing deal with the Capitals, to be paid over five years. That three year contract with the Caps was the largest ever awarded to a female athlete in Australia. It still wasn't as much as I would earn overseas, but it meant I could stay and play professionally in Australia, and I wouldn't need to work outside of basketball. I hoped it would mean more contracts for women in this country—but that's still a work in progress.

Being back with the Capitals after four years away was incredible, I loved it. I had come back mid-December, a little over halfway through the season, with ten games left to play. The Caps had won seven of the 12 games already played and were aiming to make the finals. We won nine of the remaining ten games and then beat Townsville in the semi-final and Sydney Uni in the preliminary final. Probably my best overall game memory is from this time.

I knew we weren't going to get a free run at the grand final. As I recall our opponents, the Bulleen Boomers, had only lost one game in the lead-up, but we won the game and championship with a score of 75–70. I averaged 23.8 points for the season and took out the WNBL Finals MVP for the fourth time. That was probably my most satisfying WNBL championship, I was surrounded by my friends, and was back in the community that I had boomed in, it was wonderful.

I'd returned to Australia injured yet again, and mentally that situation felt like the end of the world to me, but coming back to play with the Capitals, everything fell into place, it was perfect. I felt safe and comfortable, I was back to my old self, and to share that major win with my team, and to be feeling that good, was the best.

■ ■ ■

Not long after, I met up for a coffee with Chris Wallace, a Canberra-based journalist and good friend. When the subject of gender inequality came up, she suggested that if I had such a keen interest I could go and study it at university. Uni hadn't really been a possibility for me in the past, but I came away thinking about it and decided to look into it. I thought Open Universities Australia would be a great way to do it, as I'd found studying my Diploma of Business Management by correspondence rewarding, so I started there. Five months after Shabtai's assassination, I enrolled in a Bachelor of Arts degree at Macquarie University, majoring in Gender Studies.

I'd been struggling with understanding power relations between men and women for years. The conversations I'd have in my own head about power and control had worsened when I was in Russia, because the whole time I was there I couldn't understand why I wasn't quite able to get away. Looking back now, I know essentially I'd been afraid. Shabtai had a lot of power—much of that came from the money and the gifts he showered on us, but also from the emotional connection, he'd truly cared for us. He was a smart man and he knew how to get what he wanted, and I hadn't ever wanted to make him mad.

The minute I started studying I started to feel better about myself, it was giving me a purpose outside of my sport, and providing a level of education I'd never had before, but it was also giving me a better understanding of my own feelings. I started reading a lot of feminist literature, anything I could get my hands on about gender empowerment and gender equality, and sexual assault and rape was a part of that. One of the books I read, *The Man Who Killed Me*, was about survivors of sexual violence in Rwanda during their civil war, and I was deeply affected by it. The women's testimonies, the sort of things they'd experienced, and that some are still experiencing, were horrific. The realisation that rape and sexual violence was such a prevalent weapon of war was shocking to me. These types of things are happening in countries around the world and we don't hear about it, which mystifies me. With all the terror in the world, racial and religious hatred, how come we're not talking about this cruel gendered sexual violence? I'd led a very sheltered life and hadn't been exposed to anything like that, I was embarking on something I knew very little about, but with study I'd found a passion for something other than basketball. That was rare.

I guess by this stage of my life I also wanted to help somehow. There was a blurb about an organisation on the back of the book, The Mukomeze 'Empower Her' Foundation, located in the Netherlands. Mukomeze helps survivors of sexual violence to improve their lives, start small businesses, find sponsors, get medical help—a lot of the women are ostracised and stigmatised in their villages because they contracted HIV from the attacks. So, I contacted Mukomeze and started sponsoring these women, becoming an ambassador. If my name helps, then that's great. No one in Africa knows me, no one in the Netherlands, but to me it is something. I've always wanted to give something back to the world, but until I heard about Mukomeze I didn't know how to. It's difficult trying to find a charity or organisation you're really aligned with, but I felt I wanted to help them.

Like most people I hate to see anyone struggle. When I was living in the US, I saw a lot of homeless people. Going to work, I'd see the same homeless person every single day, and because I wanted to be able to help them, I would give them money. I wish I could have helped more, sometimes you get overwhelmed in the moment, but I did that sort of thing plenty of times. There was a car-window washer in Canberra who was always at the same set of traffic lights on the corner of Northbourne Avenue and Antill Street, and I developed a kind of rapport with him over the years. He was committed, he worked so hard, and his job would have been physically demanding, especially in Canberra's stinking hot summer. He was there rain, hail or shine, so I had no problem dropping him a 50 on special occasions. I know that not everybody felt that way towards him, and some people were probably rude to him, but he was a nice guy. I was really sad when I heard he'd passed away.

After I became a Mukomeze Foundation ambassador, the NSW Rape Crisis Centre reached out to me—and I became involved with them as well. I did some courses there and learnt about respectful relationships, but I don't think I could ever be a counsellor, because I take too much on. Even reading the testimonies from those Rwandan women made me quite depressed for a time, I found myself thinking about their experiences and reliving their accounts, so there's no way I could be a counsellor or a social worker. My way of helping is by bringing awareness and talking about it publicly, so that's what I'm doing.

I became a patron for the Rape Crisis Centre, which changed its name to Rape & Domestic Violence Services Australia, and I went to a few events for them. I have a real interest in what the organisation does. They also do great work with the National Rugby League, teaching their players about ethical sex and respectful relationships. What they do is so important, trying to tap into sports in an attempt to change the culture, it's smart, especially when this sort of behaviour is rife among some of the different sporting codes in Australia.

Domestic violence is so prevalent in this country. Thankfully I've never been affected directly by anything like that, but I know people who have, and it's absolutely horrific hearing their stories and learning about the effects that stay with them for years.

One of my Gender Studies subjects was on globalisation, with some academics arguing the need for third world countries and cheap or slave labour, basically the need for an underclass. Some people can actually justify this social and international inequality, and the necessity of having upper and lower classes. I didn't do so well in that unit.

I went from studying via correspondence at Macquarie University to the University of Canberra (UC) and continued my degree. UC had taken ownership of the Canberra Capitals and I completed my next units under a brilliant professor by the name of Patricia Easteal. She became a bit of a confidante, a mentor as well. If you could have professors like her for people like me, we'd have a lot more motivated older students, because she was great. She's written books on domestic violence and gender equality and the law. I never thought I'd be able to study law, but she made it interesting, she helped me, supported me, talked to me and gave me a deeper understanding of the issues.

Studying this course has also given me the knowledge and the confidence to talk about it with others. When I used to talk to people, men in particular, about inequality, some of them would say back to me that I was being hysterical, I was just being an emotional woman, I didn't know what I was talking about, that conversations like these were the reason masculinity was dying. A lot of those sorts of opinions probably exist subconsciously in our society, I think that men don't actually understand what they are saying and how it could be perceived as offensive. My dad, who I love and respect so completely, made a comment one time about a sportsman who'd thrown a tantrum, saying he was 'acting like a woman'. I had to stop him and ask, 'How? How is that acting like a woman? What is it? Because he's having a tanty?'. I don't think Dad even realised he was saying that the type of disrespectful behaviour displayed by the sports-man was the way all women act. Well, no, we don't. Dad was very supportive of me as a female athlete and didn't see me as less than a male athlete, but that's still an example of the type of language commonly used by men about women. I know he didn't mean to say it, he doesn't really think that the player acted like a woman. That certain player was just acting like himself. Hopefully by picking men up on language like that, we can start to change how men think about women in society.

When Julia Gillard became our first female prime minister, it really surprised me that the media focused on her appearance every day. I just wanted to know why Gillard, why women in general, were judged differently from men. For me, it went back to the whole bullying thing, back to school, where it was okay for a girl to be called a slut. Why is that okay? Women seem to be constantly assessed by the way they respond and conform to 'accepted' societal values. In comparison with men, we're judged on everything, including the way we behave, look and act. Why does it have to be like that? Just because it's the norm? We're brought up to fit into a society whose laws, whose reality, are constructed within a patriarchal framework. Continuing inequality in the workplace and the wage gap between men and women are indicative of just how far we are from being considered equal.

The biggest gender pay gap I've seen is definitely in sport. I was really lucky as a basketballer that I was able to make a living, but I had to go overseas to earn enough to save and sustain me even remotely past retirement. In AFL, cricket, soccer, there are now many avenues for women to achieve professionally, but it's still not a lot of money. A $25 000 deal isn't going to pay their bills even in their day-to-day lives while they're playing, and it's not going to sustain them post-sport—whereas men tend to be paid more, and can make a living from it. To be the first pick of the WNBA draft in 2001 was US$45 000, first pick in the men's NBA draft, we're talking millions of dollars. It's ridiculous the sort of cash that is there for men, but for women it's like, 'Oh well, women's sport, they're not as good as men, they have to start somewhere'. I know for a fact that not too many men would be able to beat me in one on one, or in a three-point contest. I bet my shooting percentage would be better than most, maybe not LeBron's, but then again, neither would most! Inequality if ever there was.

30

...

Perfect Storm

You can so easily make yourself sick when you're unhappy. Back playing in the WNBL for the 2009/2010 season, I was in better shape mentally, my body was coming back, I was healthy. I was training again at the AIS getting super-fit and I was in a great place. That season was when I first met a young up-and-coming player on the Capitals team, Abby Bishop. We just clicked and became friends straight away, she's an amazing person. Abby earned a spot on the 2010 Seattle team, she was very young then, only about 21. I was really happy knowing she would be joining us as I headed back to Seattle for my ninth season.

Lisa Leslie had retired at the end of the previous season. We'd had a chequered history, but she certainly wasn't my toughest opponent. The players who were the hardest for me to compete against were big, agile and strong, really strong—someone like Sylvia Fowles, who came into the WNBA in 2008, was very difficult to play against, because she was all those things. With Lisa, she'd been strong, but it was an even battle between the two of us. However, with Sylvia, who was my height but so much more powerful—and the woman could move, too—I had to really be playing my best basketball to feel like I'd won that battle. Truth be told, I can't actually remember ever feeling that way after I'd played against her. Other bigger players in the key had tended to be a lot slower up to that point.

In the US, Sylvia was definitely the toughest, one of the best I played against. In Australia, my toughest opponent would depend on the different stages of my career. When I was young it was probably Jenny Whittle, Trish Fallon and Rachael Sporn, then as I got older and more experienced I became quite dominant because I was so much stronger, and I was bigger than everybody else, the girls just don't have the height here. Perhaps Suzy Batkovic, we're the same age, we're very good friends, she's a left-hander, and she's always hard to guard because she can get any shot off, shots that you thought had no hope of touching the hoop, and the girl would knock them down! It was also hard playing against Suzy because I'd be in fits of laughter the whole time, we'd always be cracking up about something, on the court, on the bench. Suzy and I only needed to look at each other in a meeting and we'd burst out laughing about something we both noticed or thought of. When we're together she just makes me laugh, and she's the only player who can do that to me. I remember times when Anne Donovan was our coach in 2005, she really didn't enjoy the dynamics of the two of us, we weren't easy to handle, but we did have a lot of fun, and then again in 2009 with Brian, but Brian just thought we were lunatics, he would have a laugh with us, at us, because we were acting like ten year olds. Suzy is still playing strong, and I'm really happy for her, she's ruling the courts here in Australia, it's awesome to watch and she deserves it.

■ ■ ■

I went back to Seattle, and that year I had this thing about changing my hair colour. I can be quite an introvert, but I'm also pretty eccentric, do crazy spur-of-the-moment things at times, and that comes out in my basketball play as well. It works.

Sometimes I feel like I need a change, and I went through this phase of dyeing my hair different colours, I just wanted something different. I'd had a relationship break-up the year before, and although I hate to stereotype myself, the minute I started feeling like me again I was ready for a change. My hair's been red, it's been black, a purple streak for International Women's Day, and then when Julia Gillard became prime minister I dyed my hair bright red. Julia Gillard, I was so proud to meet her through basketball. I met all the Australian prime ministers in office when I played, but I think she had to put up with a lot of sexist crap, which was highlighted by constant personal attacks, and I believe she did well. She certainly wasn't treated as well as she should have been.

I remember wanting to colour my hair from when I was a kid. I'm a dark blonde naturally and always wanted to lighten it. Mum and I were at the supermarket, I must have been about 11 or 12 and in my first year at Murray High and I pleaded, 'Please Mum, I want to bleach my hair', I don't know how I justified it to her but she let me do it. We went back home and she helped me put it through my hair, but before we'd finished we'd used the entire packet, so she had to go back to the supermarket and get a second. Nanna Bennie was there and after I'd washed it out my hair literally turned white, I thought it looked awful. I walked out and showed Nan and I remember her telling me, 'It's alright darling, you look like Madonna!'. She was trying to ease my fears, she was such a beautiful person. The next day I went to Murray High wearing a hat, and when I took it off, people just laughed, it was like putting another target on my head. Mum called around trying to make a hairdresser's appointment, and then came to the school to pick me up and we had it fixed that afternoon. I ended up going back to a platinum blonde colour when I went to the AIS.

Abby Bishop dyed my hair red the first time, but it kept washing out and I'd end up with light pink hair, so I went to the hairdresser to get it done properly, and it came out fire-engine red. Personally I didn't like it, but once I'd committed to that colour I had to endure it because it was going to be a hell of a process getting it back to blonde. The owners of the Storm hung this huge poster out the front of the locker rooms showing the Red Queen from Tim Burton's film *Alice in Wonderland*, and I thought it must have been there for a kid's game or something—it wasn't until it was pointed out to me that I realised it was there for me! It was pretty funny.

I kept dyeing my hair, I'd get sick of a colour after a week and I'd bleach it back to blonde. My hair was coping well for a long time, and then it just started snapping off, so I had to stop. It's fine now, but I won't be doing too much of that anymore, I'm slowly getting it back to something close to natural.

Towards the end of that WNBA season my Achilles started getting bad again, but that was to be expected because it had been slowly getting worse year in year out. The more I played on it and the older I got, the worse it became. Mentally I was better than I'd been for years, and during the season I'd been playing well, my teammates were wonderful, I remember developing friendships with girls I'd played with for years but didn't really know, which just made that particular season a dream, it gave me the opportunity to really get to know them.

I did have a bad concussion halfway through the season, I'd been hit in one of the games, an elbow or a fist, playing against LA. I was knocked out, not cold, but I was definitely dopey, I don't remember too much about that period at all, but after that they wouldn't let me play until I'd fully recovered. Concussions were really being highlighted in American sport at the time. There had been a few instances in their NFL, and sporting organisations were taking a serious look at the way the injury was being handled, for the better. I definitely had symptoms, they were very aware of not letting me play through that, which was a first for me, not playing through an injury, but you can't really do that with concussion anyway. All up I was out for eight days or so, and even though I'd been named again in the All-Star team I had to miss the game.

As the Storm headed towards another championship playoff, the media were ramping up the possibility of a third MVP title for me, and just before we went to play the Western Conference championship I found out I had it. The media were calling me basketball royalty, saying that I'd joined the ranks of Sheryl Swoopes and Lisa Leslie by winning three WNBA MVPs, and wanted press statements. It was an honour for sure, but that WNBA season had just been such a wonderful year, with beautiful teammates, brilliant coaches—everything really clicked for us, the planets all fell into line, and despite taking out the MVP I simply wanted to win another championship for Seattle. That was my main focus.

Our Western Conference championship was against Phoenix that year, and we won at home 82–74 in the first game, but it was the best of three. We were a great team, we played well together, we had great chemistry, everything was working. We arrived in Phoenix for the second game and were playing terribly. Meanwhile, Diana Taunasi was having the game of her life for Phoenix. One particular play, she was bringing the ball up the court in the third quarter—she played point guard occasionally and I think Sue Bird was guarding her—when Sue fouled her. Diana had just thrown the ball at the hoop from midway down the court, because sometimes the referee would say she was shooting, and she'd get three free throws if that was the case. In fact, Diana was given the free throws, and as a competitor I was mad that they gave her those shots, because no one in their right mind would actually shoot a basketball from that spot on the court at that particular point in the game. The first free throw went in, and she had three points from her field goal. This put us 12 points down. I remember thinking to myself 'Of course she made that damn basket, could this game get any more perfect for them!', but as a vet, I also remember thinking 'She is bloody SMART!'. I was certain we were going to lose that second game, we were so far down and they had the momentum up to that point, and we were now in the fourth quarter. But, all of a sudden, we turned it around and our team just started playing. Everyone from our team on the court just played their role, Tanisha Wright played brilliant defence, Swin Cash did all the little things so well and came up with huge rebounds for us, Sue hit big shots and led us into the comeback, Camille Little was just solid, she demanded to be guarded, moved well and made some big plays—that was the best team I ever played on, we just worked well together. We won that game purely because we complemented each other and we went back to basics. For just the second time in the Storm history, we were through to the WNBA Championship.

The finals were to be the best of five games, but because we'd played so well in the regular season, we had home town advantage and were playing at KeyArena, which was absolutely packed. In a regular season game, we'd have maybe 7000 to 9000 fans there, but at the first of three final games against Atlanta Dream we had an attendance of over 15 000, and the atmosphere was electric. The scores were level at half-time, but we came out in the third quarter and clawed back the lead, I landed a three-pointer late in the quarter and we led by six going into the fourth. Atlanta came back, and with less than three seconds to go the score was tied, then Sue made a jump shot from the foul line and we were ahead 79–77. The ball changed over and an Atlanta player made a last-second try for the basket but missed. We won the first game and the fans went wild. Two more games to win for the championship.

The second game was two days later, again at KeyArena, and we won a rough and tough game, winning by three points, 87–84. One to go, this time in Atlanta. It was another rough and ragged game. We led by four points at the end of the first quarter, but were down by one point at half-time, to lead by seven at the end of the third. Atlanta came back in the last quarter, scoring 24 points to our 20, final score 87–84. When the final buzzer went, the stadium went wild, the players were ecstatic and I found Sue and hugged her, not wanting to let her go. The combination of Sue and I playing together worked, always did, and people had expected a lot, as they should, because we could do it. After the terrible end to the 2009 season, where I'd had to sit on the bench, medicated up to my eyeballs because of my back fractures, winning the championship in 2010 literally brought me to tears. Just 12 months before I honestly hadn't known if I was going to be able to come back like that.

It had been six long years since the last championship, a lot had happened, and Sue and I were the only team members left from 2004. All season long we'd been in situations where we were down points, and all the players had stepped up and hit big shots. That was the way of the team that year, a great team and incredible chemistry between players. I'd scored 26 points in each of the first two final games in the series, then scored 15 points and nine rebounds in the last game, and was awarded MVP of the finals as well as the MVP of the season. Everyone on the team played a huge role, but to go through a tough journey with someone like Sue and win at the end, you never forget that.

I'm still on a group chat with Sue, Swin, Camille, Tanisha, Ashley Robinson and Le'coe Willingham from that team, we speak daily, about everything, those girls are my closest confidantes. I know that no matter where we are in the world, no matter what time, I can get on there just to say 'Hi', or talk through any problem or any ideas, and they will be there.

31

...

The Arena

After winning the WNBA Championship we had less than a week to the 16th FIBA World Championship for Women, and Abby and I had to fly to the Czech Republic to meet up with the Opals. We'd won gold at the previous world championship four years before, and we wanted to win again.

It was a different format from previous world championships, with 12 of the 16 teams progressing into a second round-robin stage with two groups of six, meaning we would face our old nemesis the US before the quarterfinals, far earlier than any other tournament. But even if we lost to them, we could still meet them in the gold medal match if we won all our other games.

We arrived and met up with the Opals, who had plenty of new faces and a new coach, Graffy. We had time for just two training sessions together and then we were playing against Canada in the first round, which we comfortably took out 72–42. The following day we played Belarus, winning 83–59, and then beat China 91–68. We made it through the first round robin unbeaten, although I had some concern about my Achilles as I was having trouble getting around on it. But I kept playing.

We then played the second round and won against Greece and France before facing the US, who'd also made it through unbeaten. We lost against the US 83–75, but teenage Opals player Liz Cambage gave them a scare, scoring 28 points and seven rebounds. Liz stands at 2.03 metres (6 feet 8 inches), and at 19 was, and still is, a formidable centre.

Coming second in our round to the US we went into the quarterfinals against the host nation, the Czech Republic. The Czechs played out of their minds, their president came to the game, and in front of their home crowd we lost that game, 79–68. I didn't play a good game, and it was disappointing, I averaged less than 20 per cent of my goal attempts, getting just 13 points for the game, but Liz came in and took up the slack, scoring 22 points for the game. Our chances of a medal were dashed. It was a day of upsets, with world number two Russia also being beaten 70–53 by Belarus.

We had to take on Russia next. If we won we would progress for a chance at fifth or sixth place, if we lost we would be seventh or eighth in the world. It was a rude shock after taking out gold just four years before.

We managed to down Russia 78–73, but it was a tough, tight game, and we only managed to pull away decisively in the final quarter. We were playing France again after they had defeated South Korea the following day, and beat them 74–62. We came in at fifth place, despite only losing two out of nine games, but the crucial game we lost was in the quarterfinals, so we weren't able to progress.

There were a lot of younger girls coming through into the Opals, and we'd had little preparation time together. Prep time is very important, you get to know the plays, the coach, the other girls. I knew Graffy of course, but a lot of girls hadn't played under her before, it was just one of those things.

That was a really interesting year for me personally, from the high of another MVP and taking out the WNBA championship with a team who worked together when it counted, to the Opals with a new coach and a completely new team at the Worlds. It was a reality check for sure. The Opals weren't as good as we'd once been.

■ ■ ■

After Shabtai died, his wife Anna had taken over ownership of the team, but there was not as much money. I went back to Russia for a season, but I was doing it on my own, without Sue and Diana. Diana had signed a contract elsewhere and Sue wasn't coming back until after Christmas. I spent two months alone in an apartment playing EuroLeague with Sparta, and my Achilles got really bad. When I came home for a Christmas break, I had a MRI and they found a partial tear.

I returned to Russia so they could see my Achilles injury and make their own decision, and we decided that was it, they would dissolve my contract. I think because of the money I was on and their lower cash flow, Sparta were happy to let me go. I've never been back to Russia.

I came home to Albury to find that the local council were talking about renaming the Albury Sports Stadium the *Lauren Jackson Sports Centre*. The same stadium I'd grown up in and played in, that my mum and dad had played and coached in, the site of some of my proudest sporting memories. I'd even caught chicken pox in that stadium. The idea came totally out of left field, I hadn't expected it, and would never have thought about it happening, but I felt completely honoured. When they told me it was even a possibility I felt so proud, not just for me, but for Mum and Dad who had done so much for the sport in our town.

Albury was where I'd grown up, I love the lake, the city, the people, it has always felt like home. When I was first in Russia I'd said to my family that I wanted to move back to Albury, and I finally found the perfect block of land right on the lake to build on. I needed to find my own space, a place of my own, put down roots of my own. I spent so much of my time travelling for work, going from country to country, and even Sydney wasn't home for me. My apartment there was like a little dark cave. It was still lovely, an old warehouse loft, but I needed to be in a place where I would not feel dark and depressed—I needed light and space. I came back to Albury, found this block of land and decided to build a house. I designed it myself, with lots of light, space, views of the lake, somewhere to feel safe. Mum and Dad helped supervise the build while I was overseas, and I knew it would take time, but I had my own home to look forward to. People often ask, 'Where are you based, Melbourne or Sydney?', and when I tell them it's Albury, nobody gets it, unless they're originally from the country.

When it was finally decided to rename the Albury Sports Stadium I was back playing in Seattle, and my initial thought was that I wished Nan Bennie had been around, she would have loved it. It was decided I'd officially open the newly named stadium after my return from the 2011 WNBA season.

Our first game of the season gave us one last opportunity to celebrate our 2010 championship win, each player receiving a piece of jewellery, a special commemorative ring, and the club raised our second WNBA title banner to the rafters for the thousands of fans to see. We went on to defeat the Phoenix Mercury 78–71, but the cold reality of WNBA basketball hit us in our following game against Minnesota Lynx at KeyArena. Lynx scored the game's first 22 points, and by the time we recovered with a furious fourth-quarter rally it was too late, with a loss of 81–74, the first home game we'd lost since 2009. We won the next game against

Indiana at KeyArena, but travelled to LA and had a horrible game against the Sparks, the score blowing out 74–50 to LA. Two days later we were playing against Tulsa, and I'm not even sure how it happened, but midway through the game I remember going over to the coach in a huge amount of pain and saying, 'Brian, you need to sub me out, I feel like I've torn my groin in half'. He subbed me off, and I went to the locker room thinking I'd just torn a muscle in my groin. When I had some scans done back in Seattle I discovered I'd actually torn my left hip labrum. The labrum is the ring of cartilage on the outer rim of the hip socket, and it acts as both a cushion and a rubber seal, holding the ball at the top of the thighbone in the hip. I'd completely torn it off. I could hardly move, so I had surgery on it in the US rather than coming back to Australia.

Mum flew over straight away and she looked after me for two or three weeks following the surgery. The way they treated my left hip was apparently different from the procedure in Australia, and my entire left leg was black with bruising. When I woke up from surgery I was in more pain than I'd ever had in my life—and that's saying something, I thought I'd already been in plenty of pain from injuries. The sight of my black, bruised left leg was frightening, and made it worse for me to cope with.

After winning the WNBA Championship the previous year, the team were asked to the White House to meet President Obama, but I couldn't go because of the surgery. One of the owners of the club asked him to write a letter for me, which Mum has framed in her house. It was sad not to go to the White House, but pretty special getting that letter.

The girls kept playing while I rehabilitated back in Seattle, trying to get well for the playoffs. I was out for a total of 20 games before finally returning at the end of August. I felt enormous pressure, and put enormous pressure on myself to get back because I'd been injured for so long. While I was rehabbing I started to feel down again, all I could think about was playing, and the older I got, the worse my injuries seemed to get. It felt like I couldn't bounce back as well as I did when I was younger, it wasn't as easy to recover. I did make it back for the playoffs, but it hurt. When we were playing Phoenix in the playoffs it felt like the opposition were targeting my legs to put pressure on my injury, and somewhere in my head I thought, 'I can't do this, it's too much'. If I was setting screens, where I'd attempt to block or screen a defensive player away from the person they're guarding, freeing up the offensive player on our team for an open shot, they'd come into my leg and push it out—honestly, I hadn't given it enough time to heal completely, and it was so painful. We didn't make it through to the second round of playoffs that year.

I arrived back in Albury, and as I rehabbed my hip, I got ready for the opening of the renamed stadium in a few weeks' time. A good friend flew down from Sydney to chaperone me on the day, and drove me into the stadium in a really nice car, a convertible Mercedes donated by a local car dealer. It was incredible, there were over 1000 people there, and it's my home. I sat up on top of the back seat with the roof down and we drove around this one-way road leading in, past the sports centre. It didn't feel real at the time, and then when I saw the huge signage I couldn't believe it, honestly, you don't ever imagine anything like that happening, seeing your own name up there. I was honoured, completely honoured. We drove around to where they had a marquee set up, and I went over to the podium feeling really nervous, excited and emotional.

I'm an Albury girl and I think the truly emotional part was seeing my family, my friends, people I care about and love the most, in the crowd. I was sharing this honour with all of them. I was thinking about my grandmother, and almost cried. The mayor spoke, the NSW Minister for Sport and Recreation and someone from Basketball Australia said a few words, and then I got up and told them how amazing it felt to be recognised this way in my home town, and that I just never thought something like that would be possible. I was completely blown away, it didn't feel like it was happening, it was almost like I was watching it all from the outside.

I was then asked to lead the crowd into the stadium, where they had a display of my achievements—to see them all listed, with photos, the whole display was incredible. After it was over I turned to find that my whole family, including my aunties and uncles, were there, and I felt super-proud. I hadn't been able to share a lot of the special moments in my career with all of my family, so having the chance to participate in that event with them was really overwhelming. I couldn't have asked for a more perfect day.

I didn't have much time after that to spend with them, I'd signed another contract to play overseas, and was off again by the end of the week.

32

...

Spain

I'd signed a contract to play in Spain from October 2011 to May 2012. Similar to when I was playing in Russia, it was a long season, competing in both Spain and the EuroLeague. I was based in Valencia, a beautiful part of Spain, for team Ros Casares. My hip was still pretty sore, even though I'd taken time off after the WNBA season and tried to let it settle a bit. The surgeon had told me it would take a good nine months for the surgery pain to go away fully. It wasn't like I was doing any more damage to it. I was told it was sore because of the nature of the injury and the surgery, it wouldn't heal overnight, I would have to work through the pain. My Achilles was still playing up a bit, and the first few months were physically pretty hard.

I had a loft in the apartment I was living in, but I didn't sleep in it because coming down the stairs in the morning, with the combination of the pain in my Achilles and hip, was too much. There was a sofa downstairs, and I ended up sleeping on that the entire eight months I was there. I was taking a lot of painkillers to get through everything, but I still couldn't physically get up and down stairs. That was bad.

I was in Valencia, one of the prettiest places in Spain, and I hardly left my apartment outside of basketball. I just didn't want to do anything. I was getting stale, everything I did hurt. We had two practices a day, and honestly just going to practice and going on court was difficult, so I'd take yet more painkillers and get myself there, physically at least. Emotionally it can be hard when you're feeling down or hurt, and just getting myself ready to train, psyching myself up to do it, was a battle. They weren't short practices either, they were hard, my brain was fried by the end of each session.

I didn't like being a veteran, so much responsibility, and you're expected to talk to the media as well as motivate your teammates. Unfortunately, we had a major language barrier—I couldn't speak Spanish. When we weren't winning, the media wanted to talk to me about what was going on, and they couldn't understand me. In fact, when my childhood friend Sam McDonald came to visit, one of the management staff who thought she had reasonably good English told him, 'I don't understand a word Lauren says'.

Sam is a couple of years younger than me, our fathers were both presidents of Albury's men's basketball team, the

Bandits, at different times. Our families were members, our seats were always next to each other in the Albury Sports Stadium, and we grew up going to games together. He was such a cutie as a kid, he's a great guy, loves his sport, and is someone I trust, always have, he's always been there. I'd asked him to come and visit me overseas many times in the past, but that year he was in Europe playing cricket, or just doing whatever he was doing, and we made a point of meeting in Spain, and we had a ball. One evening, about five days before a big tournament, the Copa de la Reina de Baloncesto (the Queen's Cup), Sam and I had this Jameson night. I know I wasn't in a great emotional state, and I felt so relieved that he was there, and when he pulled this huge duty-free bottle of Jameson out of his bag it was, 'Okay, let's do this!'. We sat up and listened to CDs of old 1970s and 1980s Australian rock music that my dad had made for me. Music was how I got through a lot of my time overseas, I'd listen to all these Australian rock bands, all the music I love, Daddy Cool, INXS, Divinyls, James Reyne, everything, all of it. We had the music on, we had Nintendo going and we drank Jameson on the rocks—and we got through the entire bottle. I'll never forget that night, but the following day I don't think I've ever been more worse for wear in my life. I don't drink spirits. I drink wine or champagne, beer occasionally in the summer, but not spirits. I had to go to practice the next morning and I was trying to see through triple vision. I couldn't eat. I won't ever forget how I felt for the next week, I was severely hungover, so I ate a lot of greasy meals trying to soak up the alcohol, which is really just a myth and an excuse to eat junk. I was not in a good way. I probably still wasn't 100 per cent by the time we played the finals in the Queen's Cup tournament.

We'd lost a EuroLeague game before the Queen's Cup, and the club fired our coach, Nata Hejkova. Nata had coached me at Sparta in Russia, such a lovely woman, and she was one of the main reasons I went to Spain, because I knew she would be coaching that team. The team then brought in a Spanish coach who didn't speak English, and we had a lot of different nationalities on that team who couldn't speak Spanish. We lost that Queen's Cup tournament by just two points in the final, and I think our payments started to get a bit slower. We ended up winning the first national EuroLeague title for the team not long after, which made the management much happier. I don't think any team from Valencia had ever won that title, and then we went on to win the Spanish league as well. It all turned out pretty well and they got what they wanted—the championships. I think they wanted the trifecta with the Queen's Cup as well, but you can't always have everything you want.

In the last game of the Spanish finals on 24 April 2012, my other hip, my right hip, went. I had three months to go until the London Olympics.

33

...

On the Road to London

It was always such a relief getting back to Australia. The minute those Qantas jets land after long stints overseas, I'm that person who just wants to clap and cheer really loudly. There'd be times when I was playing overseas and we'd land in an airport, on another airline, and I'd see a Qantas jet coming in or leaving and it always made me so sad, because all I wanted was to be on it, going home.

Being home with my parents was just the sweetest thing in the world, Mum's cooking, wine by the ocean with my dad at their house on the South Coast where they'd retired a few years before. I dreamt of those things when I was homesick in every corner of the globe. I'd decided I wasn't going to play overseas anymore, apart from in Seattle, which was like my other home, but I'd already committed to staying with the Opals in 2012 for the lead-up to the London Olympics, and I would miss the first 19 games of the WNBA season.

When my other hip went in Spain, I knew straight away. I'd managed to get through that entire season with my left hip, which was even starting to feel a little better, but my Achilles was still playing up, and then in that last game I felt my right hip go, but wasn't sure if it was the same type of injury as the other hip, or if I had just strained my groin muscle.

I had two weeks to get back for the Opals' training camp in Canberra, and then we had a tour to Europe. My hip was on my mind and aching. I met up with the Opals girls in Canberra for the beginning of our Olympic campaign, and I remember thinking that I'd just had two weeks off, I should be ready to go.

In my first training session at the Opals camp, I was again in pain, and I didn't realise it at the time but I'd torn my right psoas muscle, a long muscle running from the lumbar region into the lower pelvis. This was already shaping up to be a long few months, but my mentality was, 'Just get through it, once the Olympics are over, you can sort it all out'.

We headed to the training camp in the Czech Republic leading up to London. The Olympics were a matter of weeks away. I was in pain in so many different areas of my body, but I wanted to play, it was the Olympic Games!

When we came back to Australia, I had a scan in Melbourne and that's when they found I'd torn my right psoas muscle, as well as the labral tear in my right hip from the last game of the Spanish season. I was given a cortisone injection into the labrum to try and relieve the pain. The Opals had a tournament in Australia against Brazil and I was kept off the court for the first of three matches as a precaution, as well as having lighter training sessions. I could have played through that first match if I had to, but that would have been counterproductive to the main goal, the Olympic Games, so we decided to get it right instead of pushing through it. I sat on the bench and watched the Opals beat the Brazilians 85–64.

I played the next two matches against Brazil and we won, with Kristi Harrower achieving her 200th game for the Opals in the match played in Bendigo. Liz Cambage had been number two draft in the WNBA the previous year and was preparing for her first Olympics, and she played well. We won all three games, a good result for the Opals, and the most pleasing thing for me as captain was to see that the team improved at each game, finding the combinations and chemistry we needed as a team. We had a strong preparation, we had spent more time together as a team preparing for this Olympics than we had for any other that I'd been involved in, except maybe Sydney.

It was back to the European training facility. I don't know if you've been on planes for long periods of time and had your leg go dead, numb—well, I'd been getting that in my right leg to some degree for quite a long time, probably 15 years or so, but then one day it started happening all the time. I began training, but I think because of my hip injury it led to my hamstring playing up, it felt like I'd turned 30 and my body was caving in. My body was seriously shutting down, I'd been going for a long time without a break from play, and even if I did have a bit of a break because of an injury, I was still constantly rehabbing to make sure I came back in relatively good shape. I'd taken the Spanish contract because I'd decided to build my dream home in Albury, and I was trying to pay it off, I felt like I had to reconcile everything. I was willing to do anything to get it all paid for, and instead *I* was paying the price, as my body steadily deteriorated, one injury leading to another.

My last stop before the Games was a couple of tournaments in England and France, playing against Great Britain, France and Angola. With my ongoing hamstring and hip injuries, I went ahead of the team to the athletes' village in London. The rest of the team had taken the Eurostar across the English Channel to France, where they played Brazil, China and our hosts, France. After defeating China and narrowly beating Brazil, the Opals lost to France 64–58. We were all still feeling confident going into the Olympics, but the French team were getting very strong.

The three silver medals I'd won at the last three Olympics were fantastic, hard-earned achievements, medals I cherished at the time and still do. The thought of winning gold was always our over-arching goal, but we had to take it one game at a time because, more often than not in sport, if you look too far ahead you are bound to be upset.

34

...

London Olympics

When I arrived at the athlete's village I found I was once again sharing a room with Liz, which we'd requested, we thought it would be a good idea and we did get along. Graffy was our team coach, with Brownie one of the assistant coaches, it definitely felt good having him there. Apart from the injuries, I was in a really good place emotionally, I was happy. My uni studies were going well, I was spending more time at home, and I thought my overseas stints were over—other than the US, but Seattle felt like home at that point.

I was sitting in my room on my own before the rest of the team arrived and someone, I can't remember who, came and told me I had to go and see the chef de mission, Nick Green. My immediately thought was 'What have I done?', maybe it was because I wasn't wearing our Olympic-issue shorts that I hadn't been issued with yet. I had no idea what I could possibly have done wrong.

I arrived at his office worried, and he asked me if I could keep a secret. I was surprised, I wasn't in trouble? Then he asked if I would like to be the flagbearer in the opening ceremony. I was stunned, and I think I said something like 'Do you have the right person, are you sure?', and when he nodded, I couldn't breathe, I didn't know what to do or say, but there is no way I would have refused. It was so surreal, I would never in a million years have thought that would happen to me, that this sort of honour could be bestowed upon me. I still don't know how it happened. I somehow managed to agree, and then I was told to keep it a secret, I couldn't tell my parents, I couldn't tell anybody. Like most things in my life, when I become overwhelmed with emotions, in this case ecstasy, I shut down outwardly, but inwardly it was multiplying inside me. I couldn't speak about it, and I thought I was going to explode.

The Opals arrived from France and I was still in shock, so I don't know if I said much to anyone. All of my teammates were saying things like 'What's going on with her?'— I was being so coy, and I just couldn't function properly. Before the announcement I was in my room with Liz, who kept asking things like 'Why are you putting on makeup?', 'Why are you doing your hair?', and then another one of my teammates walked in and immediately said 'Something is going on, what is happening? Are you the flagbearer?'.

I remember muttering that I couldn't talk to her, and so I think my teammates had cottoned on, just because of my behaviour. I guess, too, I couldn't take the smile off my face, and they all knew I was injured, which is a strange combination leading up to any tournament, let alone the Olympics. I was smiling incessantly, with injuries.

Before the start of every Olympics, there's a gathering attended by Australian athletes, officials and some famous Aussies. John Farnham, James Packer with his then wife, actors, musicians, all those sorts of people came together to celebrate with the athletes and say good luck. It's normally held the night before the opening ceremony, and that's when they traditionally announce the flagbearer. I was terrified, so nervous, I just wanted the night to be over.

My parents were on a Qantas flight to the Games when it was announced in London, and apparently the pilot told everyone over the PA. They brought champagne over to my parents, and Mum was crying. I was sponsored by Qantas, I was one of their ambassadors for the 2012 Games, which was awesome because that gave me automatic upgrades travelling with the national team. I believe in the brand, Qantas is the only airline I feel safe on in the entire world, and normally it would be Qantas jets flying me home after these long stints overseas. For me, Qantas became synonymous with joy and happiness, they took me home! I've had plenty of sponsors and affiliations with companies over the years, Nike, Samsung, Qantas, all throughout my career. They'd approach my agent, but I always tried to align myself with companies that I believed in, and Qantas was certainly well up there.

At those Games, there was a big gender inequality issue for our female athletes, and it involved travel. The male athletes were flown over in business class, and we weren't, we had economy tickets booked. As with most of our flights, you'd have to try and get an aisle or exit seat just to fit. When you're someone like Liz at 2.03 metres, or me, or any of the taller athletes, you just don't fit in those seats, let alone having to get through a 20-something hour flight. It felt like we didn't receive the same respect as the men, and that was being shown to all.

The media made a very big deal about the fact that the men flew business and we didn't, the public got behind us and thankfully that's changed now. Back in 2012, I was lucky—being an ambassador I was automatically upgraded and managed to get some, but not all, of my teammates upgraded as well. Thank you, Qantas.

Once they announced that I was carrying the flag, I didn't have to pretend anymore. As I led the team in, I was overwhelmed with emotion and on such a high, and having my teammates there, it was just lovely.

When I had marched in behind Andrew Gaze at the Sydney Olympics 12 years before, I could never have imagined I'd one day be in his position. Being the flagbearer at the London Olympics, and having my hometown stadium named after me, would have to be the two proudest moments of my career.

■ ■ ■

Two days after the opening ceremony, we played our first game against the host nation Great Britain and won 74–58, though I came off limping and exhausted.

The following morning, we played France. We were three points down just before the buzzer, and right before it went off, Abby Bishop passed the ball from the opposite end to fellow vet Belinda Snell, who shot an amazing basket from nearly three-quarters of the way down the court, straight through the net. It was huge. We were tied and the game went into overtime. Five minutes later, we lost 74–70. We went from the high of Belinda's shot to just not being able to follow it up. We'd made it through the gold medal match undefeated in the last two Olympics, and now we'd lost in only our second game. Losing that game meant we would have to cross over and play against the US before the gold medal match.

We went on to beat Brazil 67–61, then Russia. It was another tight one, and we won 70–66. During that game Lizzie became the first women in Olympic history to dunk the basketball, and it was done so gracefully and with so much ease, which was totally amazing. In the next match we beat Canada 72–63, and came out second in our round, with France on top. The US were in the top of the other round, unbeaten. The high of being at the Olympics was getting me through this tournament, and so were my after-game catch-ups with my parents at our favourite little restaurant right outside the village. They were there for me, to debrief, give me advice, and also just to escape to, if only for an hour or two, away from the craziness of the village and the Games.

I was invited by the Australian Olympic Committee to meet the Duke and Duchess of Cambridge, 'Wills and Kate', with a handful of other Commonwealth nationals, which was pretty surreal, but Mum and Dad had the opportunity to share that moment with me too, and that was so special. We talked to them for a moment and took a handful of pictures, he made a joke about my height, highly original, I told him my dog was named after him although, truthfully, he was named after my pop, William.

We were set to play the quarterfinals against China and led the first quarter 22–16, but they came back in the second, scoring another 20 points to our 17. The Opals were ahead by just one point at half-time before a scoring blitz by Liz in the third quarter lifted us to a three-point lead, and then on to a final score of 75–60, to make it into the semi-finals, against the US.

We needed to beat the US to make it to the gold medal match. We were up by two points in the first quarter and then four points by half-time—thanks mostly to Liz, who scored 19 points in just 20 minutes, she was just brilliant— but the US came out after half-time all guns blazing. They had to change their defence and moved into a zone defence, because individually they could not guard Lizzie in the paint, she just dominated. Had the game kept going in that direction we would have been on our way to the gold medal match once again. The zone changed the momentum of the game, and the US eventually ended up pulling that game out 86–73, although the score was in no way indicative of the game. Strategically, the US had outplayed us. It was a very close match, probably the best we have ever had against the US in any Olympic tournament. We were feeling down, of course, it was upsetting we hadn't got through to the big game, but there were some really positive signs, we'd played well together.

We picked ourselves up to play for bronze against Russia. They'd been beaten 81–64 by France, who were now in the gold medal match against the US. Before that match for bronze there was definitely the thought that we could come away with nothing, which would have been a huge disappointment. I'd played with or against most of the female basketballers at the Olympics, at some point, we all knew each other. I'd competed against many of the girls who were now representing Russia when I was playing over there, and I knew they were a strong team. The Opals had a pretty good track record against them during my tenure. Russia were always a bit of a thorn in the side of the US, but we always seemed to have their number for whatever reason. I wasn't overly confident before the match, but I knew we could beat them.

The Russians came out hard and fast, and by half-time we hadn't played that well, they were strong. Kristi and

I weren't going to lose that game, we weren't going to walk away from what could be, for both of us, our last Olympic Games, without a medal, and both teams probably played the best game of our tournament. All of us wanted that medal and we beat Russia 83–74. I will never forget the way I felt after that game. I was so proud of my teammates and so happy I got through the tournament—playing that game on what felt like one leg.

I know we only got bronze that Olympics, but we'd stuffed up during the rounds, losing to France in overtime, it happens, you win some, you lose some. We were pushed out in the semis by the US to play for bronze, but some of the best games I've ever played were in the Olympics, because of the stage I was playing on and because I was so passionate about representing this beautiful country that I love so much.

I don't think we'd ever have said we couldn't beat the US, but they have so many good players, the sport is huge over there. The US always had a problem with Russia because of their size, and we finally got big, but weren't at our prime at the London Olympics. I think for the Opals Liz Cambage was and is a bit of a weapon for us. That girl, if she wanted to, could lead the Opals to great heights.

For me, Sydney and London were my favourite Olympic experiences. At my first Olympics, we were playing at home, my grandmothers were both there, it was incredible, and then by London I was 12 years older and I knew what to expect and what was going to happen. In London, we came third, but I had the time of my life. Playing was hard because of the pain, but mentally and emotionally I was in a great place. I'd been able to spend time and debrief every day with the two most important people in my world, my mum and my dad, and I wasn't too distracted with the hype and the craziness that is the Olympic Games, the village, the athletes. I played in all the games at the London Olympics, I got breaks and it was fun, despite the pain. The other thing is that we didn't lose the gold medal, we won the bronze— and that felt like winning a gold medal. We'd won the last game we played at that Olympics.

35

...

Bursa

I was in a lot of pain after the Olympics, but couldn't stop. I had to return to Seattle, as I'd signed a three-year contract with them in 2011. I'd missed the majority of the 2012 season being with the Opals preparing for London, and still had the rest of the season to play—I had an obligation to the team.

Brian, our coach, was trying to manage me to get me through to the playoffs, but the thing was that my hamstring wasn't getting any better, it was getting worse. I missed three games. It wasn't going to get better until I had surgery on it. After returning from spending some time out trying to settle it down, I still managed to become the fourth WNBA player to reach 6000 points, in the game against the San Antonio Silver Stars.

The Storm made the playoffs against the Minnesota Lynx, but three of our team were out with injury, including Sue. In the playoffs we had one game apiece. I'd actually shot a three-pointer at KeyArena that took the second game—which we ultimately won—into overtime, but Brian knew I was struggling. By this stage I could hardly move, it felt like I missed everything I took, I was really affected by it. I couldn't make layups, I couldn't jump. The only thing I could do that was particularly physical was run backwards, that was the only pain-free movement I could actually make. In the third game, we were down one point when I attempted a buzzer beater, a shot just before the buzzer sounds, and missed. I'd always been known for my turnaround jump shot but that last shot bounced off the rim, a shot that nine times out of ten I would normally make. We lost that third game, and it was the end of the 2012 season for Seattle.

I was in so much pain, and in my head I was done. Physically, emotionally, done. I'd been that injured over the last two, three years—I felt like I was playing dreadful basketball, I was miserable. That last missed shot was just so indicative of that time in my life. Mentally I was actually in a really good place compared with how I'd been in Russia, but I went from emotional exhaustion to physical, and then on to being tired all the time, tired of being in pain.

I think I'd resigned myself to the fact that it was all coming to an end, and I wasn't sure if I was going to play for Australia ever again after London, either. I'd also reached the point where I thought we could never beat the US, in my time anyway. Maybe it was time to go. I started talking with the national team about retiring.

I was still contracted to Seattle for two more years and I had the Canberra contract to finish. I took the hamstring injury into the Canberra season, and I couldn't play, didn't play, that season. I turned up at training to show them and Graffy was just like, 'Try and run, try and jump, try!'. But I couldn't run, I knew there was something going on in there. The doctors kept injecting me with whatever they could, I don't know whether it was cortisone, anti-inflammatories, anaesthetic, I didn't ask, I just put up with it. But I know that every time they injected this one spot, the pain would go away completely. There was something there, in that one spot, but the doctors kept telling me that whatever it was they probably wouldn't be able to find it even if they opened it up, they couldn't see anything on the ultrasounds. So I kept on with the treatments, and the pain, but still couldn't play. I went to games, I supported my team from the bench, with one of the Capitals' games even being held in the stadium named after me. We lost that game, and it was pretty frustrating not being able to just get up and play.

It finally got to the point where we had to make a decision about exploratory surgery because my ongoing injury was wasting everyone's time, so in January 2013 I was sent to an orthopaedic surgeon based in Melbourne, Dr Young, to see if he could find anything. He operated and found a bursa, a sac of fluid, the size of a tennis ball, which was causing friction on my joint and pushing right on to my sciatic nerve—and he simply removed it. I walked out of the hospital on the following day experiencing no pain other than the wound pain from the surgery site, rather than that constant deep pain. I felt so good. I had my leg back, I could play again! My Storm contract had been suspended because of the injury, and although I'd told them that I wasn't coming back the next season they retained the rights to contract me. I'd still have to rehabilitate my hamstring for three months, but I knew in my heart that I could get back on the court.

I was happy and relieved, but I was also pretty angry. All the advice I'd previously been given was to treat the injury conservatively, as the doctors couldn't see anything, but it would never have fixed itself. If I'd had the surgery when the injury first happened, I probably would have made it back to London in better condition than I did, played with the Storm, then with the Capitals, and gone straight back to my beloved Seattle. That advice effectively lost me an entire year of injury-free basketball.

36

...

New Goals

London had been difficult—I'd been at that crossroads of, 'Do I retire or not?'. But then when the bursa was removed I knew I would play again. My dream house in Albury, which had taken so long to complete, was finally ready to move into. Building my home was so important to me, both emotionally and physically, from now on it would be my base.

I was back in Canberra, and although I wasn't playing because I was rehabilitating my hip and hamstring, we still practised twice a week. On days off I'd head back to Albury. Every spare day I got, I raced back to my new home because I was so in love with the place.

I'd had the exploratory surgery, my hamstring was recovering, I was living in my dream house, and then I found out I was pregnant. I was over the moon. My contract with Seattle had been suspended and I was intending to go back and finish my contract with Canberra, and having kids was something I'd always wanted.

I've always been private about my life, but it's not like I've purposely tried to hide anything. As an adult I felt like I was constantly in the public eye, and I'd found it difficult to maintain a long-term relationship with a partner. I like my own space—and especially when it came to sport, I was pretty selfish in terms of that, unfortunately, so relationships came and went. I always thought that when I decided to settle down and actually be with someone all the time, it would just happen. I wasn't in a permanent relationship when I found out I was having a baby, so at 32 I was setting about preparing to be a single mum.

I started buying baby clothes, thinking about where to set up the nursery in my new home as I rehabilitated, I couldn't believe how excited I was about bringing a baby into the world. I would take my baby on tour with me both here and overseas, I knew it would be hard but I would be a working single mum.

About six weeks into the pregnancy, I made plans to drive the seven hours from Albury to my parents' house down the South Coast. I stopped to visit my brother's family on the way. After I'd arrived at his place I went to the bathroom, and I remember seeing blood on the toilet paper and thinking, 'That's weird'. As it was only a relatively small amount of blood, a light pink colour, I continued on to Mum and

Dad's. I was still worried, though, and after being at my parents' place for four or five days I decided to go to the local hospital at Moruya to get my HCG levels checked, just to make sure everything was okay. Human chorionic gonadotropin or HCG is a hormone made during pregnancy that can be detected by a blood or urine test, and even though the hospital assured me that I still had good HCG levels, something just didn't feel right, I was scared. There was something in me that made me think I was going to lose the baby. As always, I was expecting the worst—that's just me, always expect the worst, and if it doesn't happen then so much the better.

Mum drove back to Albury with me because she knew I was freaking out about it, but I was more worried about how she was handling it. I was hurting for her, so I tried to be strong through it, and I think I was. I made an appointment with a radiographer once we arrived back, just to check on everything, and when the radiographer carried out the ultrasound she straight away looked at me and said, 'Yeah, you're losing it'. The baby's heartbeat had gone right down. When she told me that I was going to lose the baby I was completely devastated. I'd already imagined holding him or her, taking my baby with me as I travelled and played, and now all of that was disappearing. My foetus was dying inside me, and there was nothing I could do about it.

Within four hours I started bleeding really heavily and cramping, that was within just four hours of seeing the radiographer. It was a really terrible, bizarre experience, and then when the foetus did pass, I picked it up and it was like a blood clot. I can't describe how horrible that was, how it made me feel, it's so hard trying to describe the realisation and horror of holding your own dead foetus, and thinking about all that could have been. Every year, around that time, I think about the whole experience, it's always in the back of my mind and I have my own way of dealing with it. That experience really took the wind out of me. With the benefit of hindsight, I don't think I was completely ready for a child, but I was still totally devastated by the loss. Miscarriage is a reality for a lot of women, but it's hardly ever talked about. It was painful, miscarriages are uncomfortable, both physically and mentally.

After the miscarriage, I was diagnosed with very aggressive endometriosis, where the tissue that lines the uterus (the endometrium), starts growing on nearby areas like the ovaries and fallopian tubes. I'd always had heavy painful periods from my very first. I didn't speak to anyone about it, I didn't get it checked, I just thought that's how it was for all women. In true Jackson form we never actually talked about it. Mum gave me a book about becoming a woman when I was 12 or 13, I think it was the same book her mum had given her, and that was the total extent of our conversation about it—I really didn't know anything other than when I got my period I was able to have children. I'd been a 'late bloomer'. I didn't get my period until I was about 15 or 16 when I was at the AIS, I didn't have to wear a bra until I was on the national team, I just developed later with everything. I'd always had heavy periods lasting a week or more, and it was always really crampy, which would start the week before my period. It certainly became worse as I got older, and when I'd go to the bathroom it was like knives going through me, that's still the worst of it.

At the time I was diagnosed I'd never heard of endometriosis, which the doctor referred to as disease. I had to go back to a surgeon, and was told my chances of becoming pregnant again were reduced because of the endometriosis. Some people think being pregnant can cure endometriosis and heavy periods, but it doesn't. I had a laparoscopy, and then within a month the tissue had begun growing back and my periods started getting bad again. After that, there was a part of me that thought I would never be able to get pregnant, I was getting older, I didn't know what the future held. So, I took more painkillers and continued on.

Not long after the miscarriage, the new coach of the Australian team, Brendan Joyce, came to my house and said they wanted me back.

37

...

China

I was on track to being fit again, I wanted to play. In early August 2013, two months before I was due to go back to the Capitals, my agent was approached by a Chinese team interested in signing me up for a year. We were still working with Canberra to try and make sure that 2013 would be one of the three years (paid over five years) that I'd been contracted to play, given I'd played only one year at that stage. There was a fair bit of negotiation with my agent, and I was waiting for Canberra to get back to me to confirm that they had the money to pay me that year. Graffy had been pushing for me to play, but the team's management for some reason kept pushing the contract back. I had to make a decision on the Chinese contract, they'd given me a deadline.

Overseas contracts weren't something you knocked back if you could help it—especially given I wasn't already playing, I hadn't played for months.

My agent had given the Caps weeks of leeway, but as the deadline approached they were still taking their time. They assured him they wanted me and said they would let us know by five that last afternoon of the Chinese deadline. Five o'clock came and went and I made a decision— I was going. Frustratingly, I got an email from Canberra a few minutes later with an excuse for the delay, but it wasn't enough. I was gone, my agent had said yes to the Chinese deal.

Graffy texted me that night to say 'Welcome back', and I had to tell her that management hadn't communicated, and I was now going to be overseas. I'd had to make a choice, and one of those choices didn't seem to take my situation seriously. Everyone had expected me to go back to Canberra, and there was a bit of a kerfuffle in the media about it, but I think my agent and I were fair in our negotiations, and did everything we said we would. To Graffy's credit, she said she understood why I'd made the decision.

I was now back with the national team, and in August I was again voted in as co-captain, this time with fellow Olympian Jenni Screen, just before the FIBA Oceania Championship game against New Zealand. There were four of us on the team from the London Olympics just the year before, and we needed to beat the Tall Ferns to qualify for the 2014 FIBA World Championship.

We flew to Auckland, and as soon as I was on the court I felt like I was back, well and truly, scoring the first nine points of the game and racking up a game-high 22 points and nine rebounds in our 65–50 win. I wasn't as fit as I could have been, and was mindful of my body after the miscarriage, but just the feeling of being out on the court again and representing my country meant the absolute world to me. It was like a breath of fresh air, with a new coach—Brendan Joyce—and a new feeling in the Opals camp, everything was looking optimistic.

Next game was in Canberra at the AIS Arena, and if we won this, we were through. Playing that game to a packed crowd was amazing, I'd never seen so many people at a qualifying match before. Belinda Snell shot an incredible five three-pointers in her total 17 points of the game, and all in the first three quarters when the game was there to be won. I had a game-high 21 points and seven rebounds, I felt I was again playing at my best and I loved it. I couldn't have imagined a better way to finish the tournament that would take us to the Worlds in Turkey the following year.

By September 2013 I was in Harbin, the capital of Heilongjiang Province, getting ready to play for my new team Heilongjiang Shenda in the Women's Chinese Basketball Association. Heilongjiang Province is right up in the north-east part of China, halfway between Russia and North Korea. Training camp started at the end of September, and I would be playing through until the end of the season in late February.

Northern China was very cold, much colder than South Korea and Russia had been. It gets down to minus 40 degrees Celsius in Harbin, and when I arrived it was like a blanket of ice had been placed over the entire city. Harbin is quite industrial, and most days the pollution was so bad that every time I went outside I would sneeze, and afterwards my nasal mucus would come out black, which was pretty shocking. Not long after I arrived, Mum and Dad called from Australia to check if I was okay, they'd seen a news bulletin about pollution levels in Harbin—they'd heard about it even in Australia. It was so extreme that I was actually afraid to go outside sometimes, on certain days you couldn't see in front of you because the smog was so thick. I was given a driver, but being driven around in smog, and on the ice, was something I'd never experienced before and pretty scary. Harbin was freezing, even the buses that would pick me up from my hotel to go to the airport or take me to games would have trouble getting through the ice. I had trouble even walking out of the hotel and on to the bus because of the ice build-up everywhere, everything was slippery, so I took a few tumbles just walking around, which was pretty funny.

Their stadiums were cold too—and big, around 4000 to 5000 seat stadiums, bigger still in the richer cities we played like Shanghai. Basketball is very popular over there, and with China's huge population there are big crowds, lots of fans, to support it. Basketball is major entertainment in the US, and it's the same in China, just not with all the lights and glamour, although they still did things to keep their large fan base entertained. I think they tried to replicate the American style, but they are two completely different cultures.

We would have to train on really cold days in duffle coats, playing five on five, up and down the court—the thick coats were restrictive, but at least we were warm. Some of the newer stadiums were fine, but the older ones, they were icy cold. I've played in the hottest stadiums and I've played in the coldest.

The other players in my team were such gentle, warm girls. They were so respectful, the way they spoke to me and treated me and everything about them was just lovely. That had been my experience in South Korea as well, my team-mates were beautiful. As for the opposition teams, I'm sure they were lovely to their foreigners as well, but they would still go after you on court, that's just the nature of the sport. I loved it, I went out and gave as good as I got, I was back playing well and really enjoying it.

None of my teammates spoke English, there were no other foreigners on the team, but we found our own way of communicating. I did have a translator, she was the only one I could talk with, so she would come to games and training. I learnt how to order what I wanted to eat and how to get around to a degree, but it was pretty strange. I had to do media interviews with my translator, and I'd see photos of the girls, teams, games in the newspapers, but I was never able to understand what was in those articles, and in some ways I'm glad I wasn't. I didn't mind not speaking the language or not understanding, because it doesn't matter how good you are or what your reputation is, if you're not winning enough games there's always going to be something in the media. Even if you're performing well, there'll be someone who's not happy. And I didn't care, I didn't have to, I had no idea what they were saying. In South Korea it had been the same, even though I was playing great basketball, we were winning, there's something so comforting in not having to read or listen to any criticism—it was my coping mechanism once again. I've been like that most of my life, which is not necessarily a good thing, but it helped when I was overseas.

The girls in my team lived in these tiny little dormitories, four of them in one room alongside one of the courts, similar to how the South Korean players lived, but in even less space. They were paid a minimal salary and were contracted to these clubs, living there year-round. By contrast, I had a hotel room, and I could eat whatever I wanted—that was until I got an email from the head doctor to the Australian team telling me not to eat the meat there, as one of the Australian cyclists had been done for Clenbuterol, which had been found to come from meat they'd eaten in China. That was frightening, my anxiety went straight through the roof, all I could think or dream about was being drug-tested, completely irrational. The Australian team later qualified the warning and said the issue was linked to meat in street food, rather than meat found in restaurants—but you know what, I was so paranoid about it I just didn't eat any meat in China after that.

In China, people would stare, openly stare at me. There'd always been comfort for me when travelling with other tall people. The greatest thing about being in a basketball team, with people who are like you, is that you don't feel isolated. At airports, we were a team in uniform, I didn't really notice people looking at us because we were in a group, we weren't there as individuals. I'm used to being the tall blonde on the court, it didn't bother me standing out like that, but off the court it was different.

Back at the Chinese hotel, especially in the evening as I was going up to my room after games, after every game, there would be people drinking down in the lobby, who I'd try and avoid. I'd often find myself in an elevator with drunken guests, usually men, they'd all be looking up at me, then they'd pull out their phones and start taking photos right in my face. Honestly, one night I responded angrily in English, which they probably didn't understand, but they would have read my body language. I couldn't handle it anymore, I thought it was so rude, the whole personal space issue was so different over there. And then in the mornings, when people were leaving, coming down in the elevator, I knew that they were talking about me. I could see them looking and laughing and I'd think, 'Come on, you really don't think that I don't understand, of course I know, I'm not stupid'. It was so blatantly rude.

By the end of December, I was starting to get a niggling pain at the back of my right knee. During my time with the WNBA I'd always get pain behind my knee, I had tests done over there and no one found anything on the MRIs, so I kept playing. I was so used to pain, it was a very familiar pain, and I just kept going. In January, I felt a crack in my knee, as if something had gone in it, and I was glad there was a break for Chinese New Year coming up, which meant we'd have two weeks off before the playoffs started. It would give my knee a chance to get right so I could play properly. It was fairly traditional for the Chinese to travel back to their families over the New Year, and that included my translator. Mum came over for the break to keep me company, and on Australia Day I remember listening to the Triple J Hottest 100 in my hotel room with her, and Vance Joy's 'Riptide' came in at number one. I was so glad Mum was there. We had no translator, because she'd returned home for the holidays, and we were in this hotel room alone, it was the middle of winter and minus 40 degrees Celsius outside. When we did venture out our eyelashes would immediately get icicles on them, it was that cold. There was no snow, it was just ice, everything was blanketed in ice all of the time. Mum and I were trying to stay fit, and so every day we would walk up and down the stairs in the hotel or do circuits of the floor we were on for an hour.

During Chinese New Year we bought some cheap Chinese red wine and drank it in my hotel room, as we watched Aussie movies including *Muriel's Wedding*, while outside, the noise of fireworks going off constantly sounded like there were bombs exploding everywhere, they were so loud and unsettling. We didn't feel confident enough to go anywhere much without a translator, and mostly stayed in the hotel. I had to order food from the menus, and even though I'd been staying in that hotel it was still interesting doing the ordering, I think I even have a photo of Mum eating chicken feet! My poor mum, having to go over there—but it wasn't so lonely with her around, Mum and I are used to being the centre of our own little universe, we love spending time together. We would play the card game 500 endlessly, and I know you need four people to play, but we managed to play it with two, we'd made up our own rules. We ventured out one day and were playing 500 in a Starbucks and the staff came over and said 'No gambling, no gambling!', and we couldn't explain that we were just playing cards—but we pretty soon got the idea that you couldn't play cards in this particular Starbucks, as they reprimanded us severely. We only played cards in our hotel room after that. China was an interesting place.

Mum had travelled with me quite a bit, especially when I had injuries, and as things got harder later in my career, she was so supportive, I couldn't have done it all without her. She didn't come to Russia much during those two years I was there, I didn't want Mum and Dad to come over, to see them and then have them leave would have been too much for me. I just wanted to get through my time there, and then return and see them in Australia.

I actually needed her there in China, there's truly nothing like a mother's love. Mum was with me when we started playing again, and she was still there when our team made it to the playoffs. As soon as I got back on court, the knee pain started up again, it was a familiar feeling, so I played through it, and played through it. I also played through because of the language barrier—the team management couldn't or wouldn't understand how much pain I was in. We were coming up to the finals and they paid me to play, and that was it as far as they were concerned. And then one day it cracked again. I knew it was bad because it hurt like hell.

When my knee went the third time, I was playing against Liz Cambage who was also contracted to another Chinese team, and I was in a jump ball with Liz. I jumped up and when I landed it cracked again, and then as I tried to run up and down the court I was in tears from the pain, but they wouldn't sub me off the court. Liz was worried about me and kept asking what was wrong. I hadn't had an opportunity to see and speak with her before the game, so she didn't know I had a niggling knee injury. My team still didn't sub me off the court, my knee was clearly gone but they kept me out there. I'm not the sort of player who would walk off the court, not since I was a child, I couldn't do that anyway, I was under contract. I found out later that the meniscus, at the back of my knee where it attaches to the bone, had pulled off and chipped my bone in the process. I was in so much pain I was openly crying, and Liz turned to my bench and yelled out to them 'She can't be out here!', but they weren't listening or understanding. I had to stay on the court for that entire first half. There was something comforting about playing against Liz at that moment, I was trying to guard her and when she pushed against me in the post, she sort of dropped her step or tried to get around me to get to the basket rather than push through me, she was trying to protect me, she wasn't going as hard as she normally would have, she knew. Someone else would have completely taken advantage, gone to town on me. She was still playing the game, but I couldn't even hold my ground, when there was any pushback in the play, my knee would be flexed and I couldn't hold it. I had torn it well and truly, I knew it wasn't good.

They eventually subbed me off after half-time and I sat out the second half on the bench. Mum kept asking why they hadn't subbed me off the court earlier, I was upset, and I knew I needed to get back to Australia to get the knee seen to. I rang and begged my agent to help, and agreed to do a fitness test for the team management, as they insisted on seeing me moving about on the court. I went out there and I was running forward, it was okay I suppose, I could have played on it, but then the minute I started sliding, defensive slides or running backwards or breaking out and running a bit faster, it would grab, and there was a sharp pain. Every time I put weight on it, it was really painful, so they saw that too. When you can't actually move sideways, you can't hide it. They agreed to let me fly home, and thankfully my agent organised a release from the contract to get me out of there and back to an orthopaedic surgeon.

38

...

Torn

I had to miss another WNBA season. Brian had left and the new Seattle coach Jenny Boucek had flown over to China to see me play. Jenny had been assistant coach under both Anne and Brian, she'd been there throughout my Storm career. She's lovely, she's very religious and has a heart of gold, she's another great friend. Jenny was sitting there with Mum when my knee went and saw it all unfold, she was shattered for me, she knew exactly what had happened, and Seattle also understood. I wanted to get a couple more championships for Seattle and end my career like an athlete should—a professional athlete who's had a career like mine should end on top of the world, on their own terms. But there's nothing you can do about injuries like that. Seattle realised there was no point in pushing it anymore, I couldn't play, that was obvious.

As soon as I got home I went to see a specialist and he organised surgery the following day. He went in, repaired the meniscus insertion—where the meniscus, a thin fibrous carti-lage, attaches to the bone—and cleaned out the bone chip. It looked like my knee was good and wasn't going to deterio-rate further. As well as my knee, my left Achilles, which had been bad for a couple of years, had to be fixed. Interestingly enough, my entire right leg, everything on my right side, from my back down to my foot, was injured. With my left Achilles being so bad for so long, I sometimes wonder whether I was putting pressure on it by favouring my right side.

After the repair my knee seemed fine. My Achilles had been fixed, and I was training to get back on court, both for the Capitals and for the Opals in the Rio Olympics, which would be my fifth Games. But I had the upcoming FIBA World Championship to play first.

When it was time for me to start training again I was cleared to do some light shooting, which was a relief. But then, while practising at home with a friend, I took a jump shot, a regular three-pointer, and felt the same knee crack again, and it all came apart. Straight back to the doctors for more tests and more surgery. When they went in to look at it, it wasn't doing as well as they'd hoped or expected, and I had torn the meniscus at the insertion again.

I rehabbed my knee but it kept swelling, and it seemed that whenever I tried to get back on court for either the Australian team or for Canberra, I would be sidelined. I always felt under the pump to come back, I hated the thought of letting everyone down. I would push myself, push myself, and then something would happen again and I'd have to start all over. My knee just wasn't right, and I finally called it a day on making the 2014 world championships, and put my energy into getting ready for Canberra again.

I ended up playing just six games in all during that 2014/2015 season for the Capitals. In mid-December, I played only 15 minutes of a game against Adelaide before coming off, and had to take the following game against West Coast off to rest my knee, but I did manage to come back and play the next five games. The last game I played for the Caps that year was against the Melbourne Boomers, we won and had to win one more game after that to get into the playoffs. But after that game, my knee swelled so much that the doctors told me that I couldn't play any more games that season, they needed to go in and fix it again. Going to practices, watching the girls train and play in the finals, was just miserable, I wanted to be there for the team, for the players. Basketball was such a large part of my life, I just wanted to get back out and play.

I ended up going to see a couple of different surgeons to get their opinion, because I just wasn't getting back to playing. I had another scan, and after yet another operation the surgeon said it was fine, I just needed to strengthen it—but the pain I was in, the way it would blow up, was different from a normal flare-up. Canberra were paying so much money to try and get me back on court, I felt such a huge obligation.

■ ■ ■

In June 2015, to my surprise, I was appointed an Officer of the Order of Australia (AO). I have no idea who nominated me, no clue. I got the letter telling me I'd been nominated and asking if I accepted the nomination just after returning from China, and I was thinking, 'What does this mean? What exactly is this, and why me?'. It was a huge honour, but who, why, how?

There was a big awards ceremony at the governor-general's residence in Canberra right before the Capitals' 2015/2016 season was about to start, and Mum and Dad were there. My name was announced and I had to walk up and stand before Governor-General Sir Peter Cosgrove. I'd first met him and his wife Lynne years before, when Peter was Chief of Army and had given an inspirational speech to the Capitals before a championship run. Lynne Cosgrove is amazing, I love her, the warmest, kindest woman, and I affectionately call her Auntie Lynne. It was extra special having Peter as governor-general present the AO, topped off by my parents getting to meet the Cosgroves. It was really lovely, having that familiarity with them, that personal connection.

I was back training with Ross in Canberra at the AIS— I'd do two to three hours a day of weight training, shooting and cardio, then I'd go to the physio. Ross knew my body really well by this stage, but the national team trainer was there too. She had to be a part of it, because of the national Olympic program and with Rio coming up. The rehab was so painful, and the muscle in my knee wasn't getting any stronger, and we collectively thought it was due to my old hip injury, because my hip was aching all the time as well. All through this period I was on really heavy painkillers, I was taking a lot of stuff just to get through the day, every day.

I was training for Canberra in November 2015, and at the end of one of those sessions I was on the sideline in tears. I didn't know what was wrong with my knee, it had blown up straight away, I'd been on court maybe 45 minutes and I couldn't keep going, it felt red hot, it was burning inside my knee, and it was sort of my last attempt at getting on the court for Canberra that season. I then tried to come back after Christmas and play. I pushed myself, but my knee was just so painful, it really didn't even feel like part of my body anymore, it kept swelling up. For nearly three months I was having to get my knee drained once a week to remove the fluid from it. My medical team would put a needle in and drain it, but every time I went on court it would blow up again, and there was nothing I could do about it. There was so much fluid in the joint and around my knee. I would still play, but the pain was unbelievable, it was so inhibiting, and it would actually take me a week just to recover from being on court.

I went back to Dr Young independently and he said my knee was really loose, and that he thought the anterolateral ligament had torn a little over the course of all the flare-ups. So another scope was booked to tighten it. When he went in, he found that I'd ruptured my anterior cruciate ligament (ACL), it was three-quarters torn. When I woke up after surgery Dr Young came to see me and told me it was my ACL, and I remember texting the Capitals folk and letting them know, and from then on, for whatever reason, our relationship deteriorated.

Graffy came to me at one stage and suggested that perhaps I should retire, and I took immediate offence, I didn't want to hear it, it should be my decision to make when I was ready. I didn't want to be retired that way, nor did I think it was her place to suggest it. I was back to my stubborn old self and I still held out hope that I would make it back for the Rio Olympics a few months away. Then Graffy said to me, 'We'll pay you out, and you can go, you're not happy'. She was right, I wasn't happy, I was miserable—it felt like my life, my identity, was disintegrating with my knee. I didn't want to be around the court and watch the team train anymore, I'd been doing that for nearly two years.

Both the Canberra Capitals and I decided to end my contract. It was seven months out from Rio, and the Australian coach Brendan Joyce still wanted me to play in the Olympics, he was so supportive, doing everything he could to help me, he threw me a lifeline to cling to when I was feeling so down about it all. I hadn't been playing regularly, I'd had so many surgical procedures, so many on that right knee alone, and all under general anaesthetic, and I still needed painkillers just to move. But Rio became my goal, I was going to play in my fifth Olympics.

I went to the coast to stay with Mum and Dad while I was recovering from the ACL surgery and decided one day to get my legs waxed. It was a Saturday morning, and a short time after I returned to my parents' place my knee joint blew up, and I thought I'd reinjured it again, but couldn't work out how. My knee was hot and achy, and it was getting more and more sore as the day progressed. By that night the pain was terrible, and my knee looked fat. All of the swelling made my joint tight, and then the pain got real. By Sunday, I thought I must have re-ruptured it or something, but didn't know how because I hadn't been doing anything strenuous. I managed to get on to Dr Young, who suggested that it sounded like I was getting an infection and that I should get back and see him. I didn't believe that was the case, I couldn't see how it was remotely possible, I'd never had an infection in my life, he must be wrong.

It was Sunday, Mum and Dad had friends over, I couldn't drive, so I just left it. I didn't want to put my parents out because they'd already done so much for me and they were enjoying time with their friends, it could wait. By Monday, I started getting sick, I couldn't eat, I was getting the sweats and I thought I was coming down with some sort of bug, and again I left it. By Wednesday, I needed to speak with the surgeon again, who was fairly cranky with me at this stage and told me to get to the AIS as soon as possible so they could look at my knee and take some blood tests. Mum and Dad drove me to the AIS, the doctor did the blood tests, and then they drove me to the house I was renting from Paulie at the time. I was there on my own when the doctor from the AIS came to the house and told me to fly to Melbourne to see the surgeon straight away, I had a staphylococcal infection. They think that possibly the leg wax around the healing surgical wound had brought on the infection, but I was the one who had left it so long, it was my fault that it hadn't been seen to before. If I'd gone on the Sunday like the surgeon had originally suggested, I probably wouldn't have needed surgery, I would have just gone on antibiotics, but I was in hospital for a week and ended up having another two operations. They had to clean it all up, my knee joint had literally turned to jelly, it was already really sore from the previous surgeries and it was taking longer to heal than normal.

I knew, there was a part of me that knew, that my career was probably over.

39

...

Retirement

On 31 December 2015, New Year's Eve, my contract with the Capitals was dissolved. It was so hard, Canberra had been such a big part of my career, it was like my second home in Australia, I'd had so many great years there where I'd dominated and played well, and I was looking forward to playing and ending my career in Canberra on a good note.

Brendan Joyce told me they would stick by me, keep training me, pay for my accommodation, whatever they could do to help me to get back for Rio. I stayed in Canberra, and Basketball Australia were amazing. I was back training at the AIS, which was super-hard as my knee was just so sore, but Basketball Australia gave me every opportunity, with a further two months of training, to see how my knee was going and whether it was improving. Every time I started running or jumping or doing anything that required more strenuous activity, my knee would still just blow up and get bad, and then something else would start hurting. Two months quickly turned into six weeks, it was obvious to everyone but me that I wouldn't make Rio.

We had a meeting at the AIS. David Hughes (chief medical officer at the AIS), Greg Lovell (one of my Australian doctors at the AIS, he was great, really supportive), my physio Tony Ward (a lovely man, he'd been treating me since I was a kid), and Ross Smith were all in the room, along with Brendan and one of my old coaches, Jan Stirling, who was with Basketball Australia. We sat around the table and the doctors told me that I wasn't going to make it back. It wasn't just the doctors who were telling me this, it was everyone from the AIS and Basketball Australia, they all had to agree on the course of action. That group of people told me my career was over. I needed them to tell me because I would have kept pushing it and pushing it and I would have had no knee left. I needed to hear that from them, because I couldn't say it to myself. They told me that there was no way I was going to make it back, and, that was it.

Everyone in that room had been with me for a very long time, knew me personally, I was surrounded by people who'd supported me my entire career, so I knew it was coming from the right place, it was the right time. Everything else, my ankles, Achilles, hips, fractured back, I'd played through my whole career, but ultimately my knee was the one thing

I couldn't overcome. You can't go through all of that and come back at my age, especially given where my body was at. I'd been rehabbing and trying to get stronger, but it just hadn't worked. I didn't want to believe it, I'd had to hear it from them. In my heart, I finally knew it was over. Part of me was relieved, and then reality kicked in.

I felt sorry that I didn't get to win those championships with the Capitals and Seattle, that I didn't get to be as successful as I wanted to be at the end of my career, that I wouldn't play in one more Olympics, that I didn't get another chance to win that Olympic gold medal for Australia. But regret? No. I had so many incredible achievements that I can still be so proud of. I'd held my own, played against and with the best in the world, and achieved so much with so many wonderful people. But now it was the end of March 2016, and my basketball career was over.

At the end of that meeting it was decided we would announce my retirement the following week, at the start of the Opals' first camp leading up to the Olympics. Brendan had stuck by me and my body right to the very end, and for that I will be forever grateful. He gave me an opportunity, just one more time, to make it back, and when I finally did get to call it a day, he's the one who had all of the girls there for my retirement announcement. It felt really special and I thank him for that. There were a couple of things he did later that I thought were controversial, like not selecting my good friend and proven best '5 man' Suzy Batkovic for Rio—I did publicly say I thought that was wrong, and I stand by that.

I will always express my opinions, and Brendan was always very good to me.

My family were at the announcement. My brother Ross was there with his wife Nicole and little daughter Laura, who I adore, Laura is the apple of my eye, and even though she was not quite two years old and didn't have a clue what was going on at the time, having her there was beautiful. As well as my family, the Opals squad were there, some of my old teammates came as well, Basketball Australia made it as special as it could have been, and they did it beautifully. Ultimately, I'm glad it happened the way it did, it was right. My head was in the right space and so was my heart, or so I thought.

After the announcement, I went to walk out. The Opals were in camp and were getting ready for practice, all of those girls had been my peers, some of them had been my closest friends in confidence, and walking out of the gym as they were all going into practice, that is when I think it hit me.

I was no longer an Opal, a professional basketballer, a part of that team, any team. For so many years I'd been the captain of the Opals, and now it was all over. Because I'd been injured for the two years leading up to my retirement, I'd already begun to feel the effects of not playing in a team, not feeling part of a team—even though I was around them, it had still been hard watching them train and play. Towards the end I hadn't wanted to be there watching because I wanted to be out on court with them so much.

As I watched them go to practice I was struggling within myself. Walking out of that gym I felt really empty, but in true Lauren form I moped for a minute and then decided I just had to move on, not think about it. My usual way of getting over things is to remove myself and focus on something else, but it wasn't going to be that easy to let go.

I had to fly to Melbourne that afternoon for a charity function I'd agreed to months before. Katrina Hibbert and Kristen Veal were both at the airport, as they were also flying back to Melbourne, and I was so grateful for their presence as I tried to come to terms with it all. I drank a lot that afternoon on the plane, and then even more when I got to the hotel. I arrived at the function and everyone was asking about my retirement, it was on all the news programs. I was still on painkillers, and I drank even more, and I think I dozed my way through that night. I answered questions sarcastically, I tried to detach myself from everything that had happened that day, but with the amount of alcohol I'd drunk I really shouldn't have been there, I do regret that now. I should have been with my family at home, around people who love and support me.

I came back to Canberra the following day, I think Mum and Dad had stayed at the house I was renting there. I'd already packed some of it up, and expected to finish when I got back, but my parents had gone ahead and done everything for me, so we all finally drove back to Albury. Albury, as always, was my sanctuary.

The next morning was really weird, for the first time in my life I woke up and there was nowhere I had to be,

I didn't even have to go to the gym. So many times through my career I'd wake up and groan, thinking I had to go to the gym, and even if I didn't go it was still in the back of my mind. Now, I didn't have to be at the gym, I didn't have to get up, I didn't have to do anything, and that kind of freaked me out a bit. For a month and a half, two months, I was a bit lost.

I had a partial knee replacement. One doctor advised me not to have it done straight away, I could wait a year and see if it healed itself. But I thought, no way was I going through that pain for another year. I was going to get it fixed and not have to worry about it again, so that's what I did. It's so much better. It's not great, but it doesn't cause me nearly as much trouble or pain as before the operation. I'd never had pain during my career like the pain I had in that knee, and that's truly saying something. I'm starting to now get an inkling of that sort of pain in my left knee, which tells me it's definitely a degeneration issue. Who knows where that's going to take me.

40

...

Withdrawal

I'd never wanted to retire from injury, no athlete does, so as much as I wanted the fairytale ending, it rarely happens. There really is no such thing as a fairytale ending, unless it's leaving after a FIBA World Championship or the Olympics and you're on a winning high, or retiring at your peak—that would be perfect, but if you retire then, you're also giving three or four years of your career away, which you'll never get back.

I always wanted to keep going, to keep pushing my body. I was injured a lot throughout my career and always felt I had further things to do, more games to play, but in the end I had to be realistic. My body had given up, even when I hadn't wanted to. At my physical peak, I'd been at my emotional worst, and then when I started to feel good again mentally, that was when my body began to break down. Perhaps that was why it was a little bit harder for me when it finally happened.

There is a very physical side effect of playing sport, and then stopping. There are highs and lows almost every day playing competitively, you get used to that, your body gets used to it. Your body releases huge amounts of adrenaline when you play, and when you stop you have to come down. Towards the end of my career I was on constant painkillers and they would tire me out, which meant I'd often sleep through those 'down' phases. As I mentioned before, after seasons overseas, or major tournaments, I'd come home and immediately go down with a cold or the flu. I wouldn't get out of bed for a week, but I'd eventually wake up out of it and start moving once more, and the cycle would begin all over again—I'd have to get ready for another season, and start preparing myself physically and mentally. There is always that come-down period, and it's very real.

It had been my lifelong dream to play for Australia at the Olympics, and after experiencing the highs of that, everything else feels downhill. You think, 'I'll never feel that again, I'll never have that elation again'. I guess that was why one last Olympics was such a motivator to try as hard as I did to come back. It's like preparing for a one-off big event, with an extended period of time leading up to it, and then when it's all over, you come down. At the end of a career, it's so much worse, that down is permanent. Your entire life as you know it just stops, who you identify yourself as comes to an abrupt end. When you play overseas, you're paid to play and that's your job, it quickly becomes your life, your identity, but I think that makes the leaving even harder, you don't have an alternative.

The minute I retired I wasn't an athlete anymore. When it's over, it's done, and normally you're a bit worse for wear physically. Emotionally, I'm lucky I came out better than when I was playing.

After the knee replacement, I was on bed rest for a month at least. I wasn't entirely bedridden—I was still pushing my knee so that I could find my comfort level moving around again. But I was on a lot of prescription drugs, and I didn't want to do anything.

I got a call out of the blue in late April 2016 from Guy Molloy, head coach of the Melbourne Boomers, saying some people from their WNBL club would like to meet me about a job offer. I knew Melbourne had been struggling, and didn't know if they were going to be in the league that year. Guy and two board members, Tony Hallam and Jim Avgerinos, came to my home and asked if I'd be interested in working for the Boomers and I immediately said yes, no hesitation. I needed to have something in my life that I could strive towards, I'd almost finished university, and I needed something to get me out of the house and moving again. It was all too easy to stay at home, stay in bed, but I thought 'No, if I'm going to do this I have to get out there', so I did. I got out of bed and got my life back together, thank goodness.

Then one morning in May I woke up and decided I needed to get off all these drugs, I needed to get off them *now*. I was drinking a lot of alcohol after the retirement, and I thought 'I cannot do this anymore, no matter how much pain it will cause, I have to get off it', and I did. I was in so much pain when I was training and playing that I couldn't have stopped the painkillers any earlier, I wouldn't have been able to move if I hadn't been on them. I was still taking the antidepressants, which had helped me through that time as well. I've talked about the roller coaster of sport, you have huge highs and lows, and the antidepressants evened that out for me. I can do that on my own now without sport, but when you're coming off those highs of playing or training, your endorphins do go crazy. I'd get really frustrated if someone called me and needed something from me when all I wanted to do was concentrate on my sport, concentrate on me. I guess it's all a part of learning about yourself and growing, and no doubt there was a lingering dependency on all that crap.

I'm really lucky that I found the strength to stop taking prescription drugs and antidepressants when I did. It showed me that I had a lot more strength than I thought I did. I just got my shit together, stopped taking pills. It wasn't easy though. Mum was with me, thankfully, when I was coming down off everything. I suddenly stopped all the tablets without consulting anyone and it was really tough, but I'd made a decision and went with it. Honestly, there were days where I thought I would have to take something, there were days where I was shivering uncontrollably, it was shocking.

But knowing myself and who I am, I had to do it my own way. I've always been an all or nothing type person. It probably wasn't my brightest idea, but it was the best thing I ever did in hindsight. I've never been clearer.

One of the drugs, Lyrica, was particularly hard to come off. I'd been on it about a year at that stage, and I couldn't understand why it was so difficult to stop taking it. I decided to Google it, and discovered that it's a very strange drug. Apparently, it affects chemicals in your brain that send pain across your nervous system, which is why it was originally prescribed to treat issues with the sciatic nerve in my back, as well as the pain in my hamstring and my knee. But in Europe, it's also used to treat anxiety, and coming off it was really difficult. I was on Valium as well, Endone for the pain, I don't want to seem like I was a drug addict, but there were other painkillers, sleeping tablets and antidepressants, I was on quite a lot.

Coming off the antidepressants was very similar to coming off Lyrica. I'd get really tingly, have heavy sweats, I mean a lot of sweat, and became very anxious. But I made it to the other side, with Mum beside me. I was so fortunate to get through that, to know that there was an end, whether it was a week away or whatever, I just knew I could get through that period, I had to, so I could move forward with my life.

■ ■ ■

My role with the Melbourne Boomers is as the team's assistant general manager, and my boss is the general manager, Justin Nelson. Justin, with the help of a board of very savvy businessmen and businesswomen, took that club from being about to fold to a complete turnaround in one year. It was unbelievable to watch. He did it with the backing of the new ownership group and some very inspired people. I'm not sure having my name helped that much, there's only so much a name can do, especially a retired one. Justin's an absolute go-getter, very smart and a really good person. I'm still learning from him every single day, he never stops, he just goes and goes and goes, and it's brilliant. I don't know how anyone can be that driven, but he's so passionate about the team and I think, for me, there could not have been a better transition out of sport into business.

I work with signing players, game-day operations, ticketing, memberships, a fairly broad list of duties, but that's where women's basketball is at in this country, you only have a few people running an entire professional club. People sometimes ask me if being around the team makes me miss basketball, but no it doesn't. I don't miss stretching, warming up, it all just hurt towards the end, I certainly don't miss that. My body was ready to retire, I was ready to retire. I was one of the lucky athletes, because I had something to go on with, I was offered an incredible job, almost straight after the knee replacement. And I had my beautiful home, too. I'm so fortunate that basketball set me up to a point where I didn't have to rely on anything or anyone post-sport.

A lot of athletes don't have that, and that's the hardest thing, there's no transitional program for them, there's nothing to help them out.

To be honest, back when I was 20 I wouldn't have wanted someone to say to me, 'It's a short career, it will be over before you know it, be prepared for it, plan for after'. I think someone may have even said that to me, but I wouldn't have wanted to hear it. I'd have been like, 'Yeah, right'. But now there is some awareness about what happens to athletes post-career, that a career doesn't last forever. Mine, as for all athletes, definitely did not.

After I finally made my way through the various prescription drug withdrawals, I was still drinking, but then I had the perfect reason to stop, a wonderful surprise. I was pregnant again. I was really scared, and as usual, thought the worst. Since my miscarriage and endometriosis diagnosis I'd really thought in the back of my mind I couldn't get pregnant, so I was over the moon to find out I was, but also cautious and protective. My parents were happy, they were really happy, but Mum was cautious as well, telling me to keep in mind that it was early days and not to get my hopes up. After what I'd been through, they didn't want me to fall back, go back into that dark, dismal place.

41

∎ ∎ ∎

Number 15

Sue Bird once told me that athletes die two deaths—the first is retirement. People might think that's melodramatic, but metaphorically speaking, it's true. It's a huge part of you that dies, when it's over it's over, and you can never go back.

Not long after retiring, my agent contacted me and told me that Seattle had been in touch and that they wanted to officially retire my jersey, the first to be retired in the Storm's then 16-year history. To have your jersey retired in the US is huge. Your number, your jersey, will never be worn again by a player for that club. It was a huge honour, especially being a foreigner over there, and having the impact I did. Number 15 had been my mum's number when she played for Australia, it was my number after arriving in Seattle, and

a few years after that became my number with the Opals.
And now Seattle Storm were willing to retire it. They don't
do that in Australia.

They asked me back to Seattle for a retirement ceremony,
and that also meant a lot, because the way my career ended
I'd never got to say goodbye to anyone. I felt like I didn't
have any closure, I'd never said goodbye to the fans who'd
been so supportive of me over the years, to my teammates,
to basketball in the US.

Going back to Seattle was amazing, it was like a time
warp, it felt like I'd never left in a lot of ways, and it brought
back all of these emotions—being pregnant probably didn't
help. Sue surprised me at the airport to welcome me back,
which was lovely, it was so good seeing her again. I'd always
wanted to get back to the US, to see Sue in particular, but I
didn't realise how important it was for me until I was there.
Sue had been such a huge part of my career, pretty much my
whole career, especially playing over there and in Russia,
and then playing against her when she was the point guard
for the US team. She's brilliant. Sue and I were unstoppa-
ble on the court, off court we'd been best friends, and we
still talk everyday online. I hadn't seen her in four years
when she met me at the airport, and yet it felt like I'd never
gone anywhere.

The way my career finished I never had a final game
that was good enough to end on, I had no control over it,
and because of that I think I'd tried to remove memories of
being in Seattle. I didn't realise how much I missed being

there until I went back. After 2012, even after my hamstring injury, I was planning on returning, but then I became pregnant the first time and had asked to take 2013 off from the WNBA. By the time I'd miscarried it was too late to return to the US, but I'd always planned to be back in 2014. But then my knee went in China, and I'd tried to get home for the Australian team. The injuries, the rehab, there was no opportunity to get back to Seattle. But now it felt so good to be there, I was so excited.

Sue and I did some media interviews and videos for the ceremony at a school and at KeyArena just after I arrived, and I was feeling really jetlagged and emotional. Thankfully, I'd arranged to come over a couple of days before the jersey retirement ceremony. Walking back into KeyArena it felt like I belonged, and it honestly seemed like it had been no time at all since my last game. I will always hold my time in Seattle as a special part of my life. Re-entering that arena, it truly hit me—I wished I was playing again more than anything.

Before the ceremony, I did an event for Seattle Storm season ticket holders, which was hosted by Nike. I got to do a Q&A and there was an autograph session afterwards. When I was playing, there'd been this little girl named Grace who started to become a fan when she was about two or three years of age, she used to wear my jersey to games. She was the prettiest little thing, a gorgeous kid, and was always at the matches with her parents. The family were members, we met season holders at events, at games, and every time we had a season ticket event Grace was there.

I always popped her on my lap and talked with her. I've never been that great with kids, but every now and then I would get clucky, not very often, but she was the sort of kid I got clucky over, she was the cutest thing. I was signing these autographs at the retirement event and I looked up and there was this tall young woman and I suddenly realised, 'OMG, it's her, it's Grace!'. She'd grown up. I started crying, I'd held it together reasonably well until then but that was what got me, seeing her and realising how long it had been, she was now a teenager, that's how long I'd been playing over there. She will forever be in my heart, I will always remember her.

The jersey retirement ceremony happened after a WNBA game between the Storm and the Washington Mystics, with the Storm taking out the game 80–51. Watching that game was hard, I again just wanted to be out there playing. I definitely felt that there was a part of me missing. I became sad with the realisation that for me it was completely over.

KeyArena was packed, and I walked in after the game to a standing ovation. I'd been their franchise player, I'd grown from a 19-year-old rookie into a veteran. I'd taken out three MVP awards, led the Storm to 2004 and 2010 championships, and had 12 unbelievable seasons playing 358 games in a Storm uniform. And now for the first time in their franchise history, they were going to retire my jersey, number 15. I was wearing Sue's shirt, I wanted to honour her as well, deflect from myself a bit, I tend to get embarrassed with all the hype. The shirt was oversized—I like being comfortable—and I didn't want to wear anything to show my expanding belly, my little secret.

They played congratulatory video messages from the WNBA president, WNBA legends and friends including Tina Thompson, who I'd first played against when I was 15 years old—she and I had awesome memories together, whether playing against each other in the WNBA and internationally or together in the All-Star teams. The CEO and president of the Storm then spoke, and there were more video messages from my three Seattle coaches, Lin Dunn, Anne Donovan and Brian Agler. I could feel the love, and the pride, as they reminded everyone what an amazing career I had there. And then Jenny Boucek got up, saying I had the worst 'potty mouth' in the WNBA, which everyone laughed at, but hey, I'm Australian. She then told a story I hadn't thought about in a long time. When she'd been assistant coach she would often get my rebounds as I practised my 1000 shot sessions, and in 2003 I stopped, looked her straight in the eye and told her, 'Bou, I want to be the best in the world'. I put it out there, took responsibility, and went on to win my first MVP in WNBA.

There were messages from fellow Aussie players, past Storm teammates, I was presented with a framed montage of photos and a huge banner signed by fans, my jersey framed for me, it was all quite overwhelming, and then Sue got up.

Sue is so good at public speaking, she had everyone laughing as she talked about our tactics and plays in games. She mentioned 'The Stare' and that even the point guard wasn't immune to it, it was apparently a rite of passage in the Storm to be yelled at by me, but I always had their backs, we were a team. She told them that for every time I yelled at her for not passing her the fucking ball, she'd tell me to 'remember the play then!'. The only plays I knew were the ones that ended with the ball in my hands, and if they weren't designed for me, I'd still end up shooting the ball when it passed through my hands. Whenever I got the ball I would shoot it, but a lot of the time it paid off. It wasn't until my retirement in America that it was brought to my attention that they all knew I didn't know the plays most of the time, unless they were for me. If my coaches weren't happy about it, they never told me. I think they probably tried to stop me doing it, but they'd rather me on the court than off.

I had two really good point guards in my career, one was Sue Bird, who was the best ever, and the other was Kristi Harrower, who was close to being the best point guard in my mind. Both of them were very good at reading the game and drawing up plays and doing anything within the play that would get people open. They can see things happening before anyone else does, and that's why I credit a lot of my individual awards to the Bird, she made me a better player. At the retirement, they said Sue and I were the best duo in WNBA history. Perhaps they were right, but I do know we trusted each other, as players and as friends. We truly complemented each other.

After Sue spoke, they had a countdown from 15, and unveiled a big green banner hanging from the rafters to reveal the jersey banner JACKSON 15. They then asked me for a few words. I didn't think I'd get that emotional until Sue started crying as we hugged. I thanked them all, some guy yelled out from the crowd that he loved me and it made me laugh, so I shot back that I loved him too. It was a special night, I wasn't sure I would ever get back to Seattle, but it was probably the most important thing I'd done since retiring.

It had been a hard four years since I'd played there, and being in KeyArena again, I was completely overwhelmed. I truly hadn't realised how much I'd missed Seattle. I was a shitty teenager when I arrived, and the relationships I developed with coaches, players, owners, trainers in my 12 years playing there had become the most memorable for me. I thanked them all from my heart.

There was a definite sense of finality as I said goodbye to Seattle basketball. Seattle Storm jersey number 15 was officially retired, it can't be used again, and that's a huge honour. It's sort of sad because it's a bloody great number.

42

...

Commentary

There's so much in Seattle that I'll always remember—being made so welcome, and the joy and jubilation we managed to give the city and its people, twice, with those championships. I will go to my death bed with beautiful memories, I had such a great time over there. America was awesome, it was hard, really hard, but it made me who I am, and I made some amazing friends over there, my American family. I had remarkable, memorable games, but honestly, the friendships are my best memories.

It would have been nice to win a couple more championships for Seattle, but I did get injured a lot, my body just couldn't handle the toll, the training and flying. In America, we would play, we would fly, we would train again and again, there were no breaks. Flying also probably contributed to my body's inability to recover, it wasn't just the emotional anxiety stuff, it was also the physical impact that flying had on me, the swelling in my feet and legs. Towards the end I wouldn't be able to walk off planes without a noticeable limp.

The day after the ceremony I had a haemorrhage. I was meant to fly back home and couldn't. I was at Abby Bishop's apartment, she was back playing with Seattle, and Suzy Batkovic was at the apartment as well, she'd flown in that day and was exhausted. The three of us were talking, and I excused myself to go to the bathroom and thought 'Holy shit I'm bleeding', and because of my miscarriage in 2013 I was terrified that I was about to miscarry again. Abby and Suzy took me straight to the hospital. We arrived and they did some tests and then an ultrasound, and I was so relieved to see the baby's little heart still beating. They put me on bed rest, saying there was a 50:50 chance that I'd lose my baby. I decided I wanted to fly back after a couple of days because I wanted to be around my doctors and my mum and dad if I miscarried again.

As soon as I arrived back in Albury I was treated by the specialist here, and then went to stay with Mum and Dad down the South Coast. I had continual spotting for another nine weeks and didn't know if I was going to miscarry or not.

With the Rio Olympics coming up, Channel 7 had asked if I would be available to do a commentary for the women's basketball. I'd agreed prior to becoming pregnant and now that I was, I didn't want to travel to Brazil because of the

Zika virus. Zika is spread by mosquitoes and can affect the foetus in pregnant women, causing birth defects including the horrible condition known as microcephaly, where the baby is born with a smaller than normal head, the brain doesn't develop properly and the child has ongoing mental and physical developmental problems. There was no way I was going over there pregnant, and thankfully Channel 7 agreed that I could broadcast from their Sydney studio.

Mum and I drove up to Sydney from the South Coast before the Olympics started, in preparation for my first commentary gig. I was driving through morning traffic on the highway through Milton and was taking a bend in the road. Someone had parked a closed-off trailer on the corner, so there was no vision through it. I was doing the speed limit through morning traffic, and Mum and I were just talking, and I thought I was at a safe distance from the car in front, I looked at Mum, and next thing I know I was up the backside of the car in front. What I didn't know or see in that split second was that the car ahead had slowed down, I hadn't seen it through the trailer, and I ran into them. It was scary, and because of everything that was going on in my body, I was in a bit of a state.

A woman a few cars ahead of the car I rear-ended got out of her car and called me quite a few names. I was in shock, I wasn't even sure what was going on. By the time I realised what she'd said to me, she'd gone, otherwise knowing me I probably would have responded. My car wouldn't start, I couldn't move it off the road. Everyone was getting mad because it's a busy highway, right through the middle of town, people were winding down their windows saying, 'Get your car off the road!', but it wouldn't move, I didn't know what to do. Mum got out in the middle of the highway and started to direct traffic—looking back on it, it's funny, but I know she was scared. I managed to call Dad and say 'Dad there's been an accident', and then hung up the phone, poor Dad. I really had a pregnancy brain, I have honestly never felt that ditzy before in my life, I forgot everything, it was crazy.

The car I'd hit ran on LPG and had a gas leak, so the police had to shut off the entire Princes Highway. The police were really lovely, when they found out I was pregnant they made sure I was okay. Clearly the accident was my fault, because I ran up the back of someone else, but apparently accidents happened a lot on that part of the highway. As fate would have it, we were across the road from the Milton–Ulladulla hospital, so after the police carried out drug and alcohol tests on me, which were mandatory, we then walked over to the hospital to get checked out.

Mum had been holding a laptop computer while we'd been driving, and when we had the accident it flew up, hit the windscreen and came down on her leg, so they checked her out. I had whiplash from the seatbelt, but my baby was okay. I felt like such an idiot, it was the first car accident I'd had, and I don't want to ever have another.

Dad drove straight up to Ulladulla and was relieved to find that we were both alright. My parents are unreal, they truly are, I have the best parents. Mum didn't leave my side for two weeks after the accident, and she was with me while I commentated for Channel 7.

I'd never commentated before, and at the start I felt uncomfortable, it was tricky even just knowing when to talk and say things. I found myself sitting there, watching and analysing the game—but in my own head, not vocalising my thoughts. Instead of watching and speaking, I was watching and making noises of annoyance, disappointment, approval, and no one could see me of course, they could just hear these noises as the game was televised. Thankfully there were two other veteran commentators covering the women's basketball who were really good, they spoke a lot, and initially I just chimed in. I was finding it difficult to vocalise what I was seeing and thinking, but what I needed to realise earlier was that people wanted to hear what I had to say, I was so afraid that what I was saying would be wrong. It was Mum who set me straight. She'd certainly noticed my lack of commentary. Mum told me to think about who I am, think about the fact that I knew more about this game than anyone there, so just speak! I did find it difficult, though, when there was a terrible play, because a lot of those girls competing were my friends. You can't sort of say 'That was terrible,' because they're your mates, so that was hard, but I guess down the track I won't know the girls as well, and it will be easier.

Being a public figure and recognisable, people want to be with you when you're out and about, they want to talk with you, there's an expectation. I think it's a familiarity people have with you, even though you don't know them, know who they are or what they want. I was walking around the Myer store with Mum on one occasion, I can't remember if I was still on crutches, but I was still recovering from the knee replacement, was off the painkillers and in a lot of pain— and I was pregnant. Mum was in the change rooms trying on some clothes and I was hobbling around Myer trying to find a shirt to wear to an upcoming function, I was just wearing tracksuit pants and a T-shirt, my hair was messy, and this woman came straight up to me with her kids. I hadn't really taken any notice of her, I was just wandering around. I don't know what she said, but I remember being taken completely by surprise at how blunt and forward she seemed, coming right into my personal space. I felt really vulnerable, and I know I didn't go out of my way to talk with her. I think I smiled, said 'Hi', and kept going. She walked off and went into the same set of change rooms that Mum was in.

Mum came out and demanded to know what ever had I said to that woman. I was shocked. Mum expects me to be polite to everyone all the time. I wasn't rude to the woman, but I didn't give her the time she must have wanted. Apparently, she'd gone into the cubicle next to Mum and went to town about me to her kids. When Mum told me, I was stunned. I saw the woman come out of the change room and I wanted to say something, explain what it was like to have a complete stranger come up and be like that, be that familiar and forthright. I didn't know the woman from a bar of soap and she expected me to talk with her and her

288

children like we were old friends. I didn't try to explain, I left it, I don't think she would have comprehended what it's like from my side. There's no point in trying to fight those battles.

I get that expectation a lot, and usually manage it, but I know I didn't handle it well that time. I think I was in so much pain I didn't want to deal with it, but I also know that I wasn't overtly rude. That sort of situation has occurred a few times, and I think it's because normally I'm fairly oblivious to things happening around me—as I said earlier, I'm so used to people staring due to my height that I just go about my business, and it usually works for me.

People in Albury are more respectful of my personal space. I can walk down the street and know people are looking at me, but I don't really get that sort of intrusion, most people understand. I walk around Albury with pride, all of my family and friends are there, it really is my safe place and I love it.

43

...

Transitioning

Sport often seems to be a bit behind the rest of society in terms of social issues. Talking about depression, homophobia, alcohol, anxiety, drugs, even bullying, any of those issues, we've tended to be behind the eight ball as athletes. There's a perception that you're a role model, you play sport, you have to be this way, you have to behave that way—you're pigeonholed.

When I was playing, I didn't openly talk about any social issues, nobody did. I had no idea what I was going through when I had my first anxiety attack on tour with the Gems all those years ago, I didn't know that it was actually quite common. It would have been so reassuring to feel able to talk with someone then, to get treatment, to get help way back when it first started. It's the same in the US—there's a tough machismo, even with the female athletes, but especially around male athletes, that means you don't discuss social issues, you just don't. Whereas broader society *is* talking. When sport takes on these issues, the rest of society tends to take them on as well, because sport is so entrenched in our culture. I used to wonder if the sporting world's reluctance to discuss real human problems came from a fear of scaring off potential sponsors, or making athletes appear less than perfect, which would be so 'shocking', and maybe this is why I didn't talk about anything until I retired. It is so promising to see athletes portrayed as humans who are just like everyone else who are openly discussing social issues now, it's real and it's honest and it will make it easier for the next generations.

After retired rugby player Daniel Vickerman committed suicide in 2017, all of a sudden, athletes in Australia were talking about life after a sporting career. I was asked to speak on two different television panels, *Insight* and *Four Corners*, with other retired athletes, about the problems that professional athletes face when retiring from sport. I wanted to talk out about athletes transitioning into retirement because that, for me, was a real problem—but I had a genuine fear that by doing both of those programs it could be taken in the wrong vein. However, it was really refreshing for me that people were so open about it on air, comforting almost, knowing that I'm not the only one who went through issues that—let's face it—anyone can go through in life. I'd had my issues with prescription painkillers and had seen fellow athletes who'd fallen into the trap of alcoholism or drugs, and decided personally that I would speak out about it. I think I had a duty as an ex-athlete to do that. Since I've started to open up about my experiences, a few of my teammates have written and told me I was brave to do it, but I don't think I was brave at all, I was just speaking about something I went through, and hopefully that will help others.

On the *Insight* program, I also talked about depression. I guess what didn't come across was that I had issues way before I retired, in particular those two years in Russia, and that I had anxiety issues outside of that. In retirement, I had an emptiness, a feeling of 'What am I going to do with my life? What do I get out of bed for?', that was not like any depression I'd previously experienced. Emptiness is probably the best way to describe that time for me, and it's what most people would go through after losing something that has been dear to them for so long, something that defines them.

Most people retire from their career at 60, 65 or 75 years of age. I had to retire and leave my passion when I was 35 and find something else, something else I was good at. Having been on top of the world for so long, experiencing those highs and then to come crashing down, permanently, I had definitely felt empty. But I, unlike many others, had been given a lifeline. Being offered the job at the Boomers gave me direction, a reason to get free from the haze, to get on with life and be passionate about something again.

On *Four Corners*, I was one of a group of retired athletes talking about life after professional sport. If you've committed your whole life to your sport, then that transition period out of sport is going to be tough. And if you haven't got anything behind you, and the majority of young athletes don't, then it's even tougher.

Being a professional athlete, regardless of how much money you're making, you're expected to pour your entire life into your sport—what you eat, how you train, sleep, treat your body, how you do everything as a professional athlete should. And that rarely leaves time for anything else. It's often very hard for athletes, especially at a representative level, to do something like study or undertake an apprenticeship to prepare for when they retire, and I think this is an area where sporting bodies could help. The institutions think they *are* trying to help, and they may view me saying something about this sort of assistance as a direct attack—but it's not a direct attack, it's just about trying to figure out ways forward that are beneficial and proactive, applicable to all. So long as we are sparking conversation and igniting a bit of change in the sporting organisations, we are getting people thinking. Doing interviews, and writing and talking about issues, are great ways to get that happening. Some people are going to take offence at what I say, someone is always going to have a problem with something, but here goes.

When I retired, Basketball Australia were wonderful, but afterwards there was no follow-through. I didn't necessarily need it, but knowing it was there would be awesome for all players. I was one of the lucky ones, I'd been playing long enough and in leagues that paid good professional wages, but if I didn't get any help from BA when I retired—and that could have just been a phone call—well, no one else is going to either. They might help during your career, and that's great, but players need it most when they're transitioning out of the game. Not everyone is lucky enough to play a sport that will help them financially, and I had to go overseas to get that. When you retire after playing a sport just about full-time from virtual childhood, you're effectively losing the only job you've ever known.

It was after my first major injury that my thoughts turned to preparing for life after my sporting career. I hadn't enjoyed school at all, but when I did the online business course I found that I studied well via correspondence. I also undertook a real estate course, if all else failed I could have started my own real estate business, I wouldn't have loved it, but I could have done it, so I always had something to fall back on if I needed to. I decided to go to university and study a subject that really interested me, and figure out a career path following on from that. I'm now so glad I did.

I certainly know it's hard to do, but if a study opportunity was there as an option for professional athletes, I think some people would take it up. If not university, then maybe a trade, or TAFE, or any sort of qualification, work experience. The sport governing bodies could help provide access to these things, let athletes know about programs or courses that the sporting bodies are aligned with—take your pick, it's there if you want to do it, or not. Once athletes get to a certain age, I guarantee they will take it up. At 25 you're a mature age student, and I know I didn't think about study until I had my first serious injury at 24. When an athlete is off with an injury, perhaps the sporting bodies could have someone come in from an organisation and put forward some options. You've got a bit of time on your hands after an injury, here are some options, why don't you have a go at one of these, or one unit of study, see if you like it? It could give some reassurance or even certainty to athletes for their future life after sport.

Hearing the CEO of Basketball Australia talking on the *Four Corners* interview was really reassuring and impressive, I'd never heard him talk like that before, saying that they need to support their athletes both on and off the court, when they're in a team and when they're not, and as they're transitioning. He mentioned building a structure over the next three to five years to do just that, and that it was a priority. It will be interesting to see if it will change, because there's currently no structure for any athlete in basketball that I know of.

Kids looking at going into professional sport need to be aware of these issues at some point, because they're going to come across this themselves. No matter what your age or your path, the time comes when you have to look after yourself and make decisions on your own, and for professional athletes where resources such as food, accommodation, health care as well as sponsorship are handed to them as they play, thinking about life after sport needs to be something considered from the start, as hard as that is initially. I played year-round as a professional basketballer, I was paid well, but the kids who play because they love it and are not getting great contracts, contracts that are worth it, I don't know how they do it.

It's interesting, if there is something going on in basket-ball I always get a call from someone in the media, straight away, people are asking for my opinion and I don't always see why. My knowledge is important, my opinion is import-ant, I guess. Now, I'll always say what I think, whereas when I was playing I tried to be diplomatic and not tread on anyone's toes. It's different, I'm not a player anymore. As professional sportspeople, we are told to be tough when we train and play, and even in retirement. Now, when I do an interview, if I delve a little bit into my life, it instantly becomes big news, which is funny because it shouldn't. I never would have talked about being addicted to prescrip-tion medication, or about anxiety and depression when I was playing, because I didn't want people to think I was looking for an excuse for why I wasn't winning or performing better. Now it's so much easier—because my career is over, they can only judge me on the career I've already had. A lot of retired athletes are coming out now and talking about issues after retirement, because when you're in your career you don't want to have excuses.

Depression and anxiety are quite common in athletes, but no one talks about it. When I was playing, I felt ashamed

I think, and I didn't want the media, the public, delving into my personal life. Anytime you open up at all, you become a target.

In response to being on those two TV programs I was contacted by ex NBL and ex WNBL players, Boomer and Opals players both current and ex-players, even people who have nothing to do with sport were emailing me, calling me, it was really interesting, they were in agreement with me and relieved that someone was talking about it. I just feel it all needed to be said, because we all go through it and no one talks about it. Now that we have this in common, we can talk about it and work together to hopefully make it easier for the next generation.

On Twitter, though, there were some comments from guys who I don't think even watched the program, I think they'd seen the commentary on social media and responded flippantly. Comments like 'We have jobs and we don't get depressed when we lose them', or 'Go and check your bank account'. I don't judge them on their lives, so for them to automatically judge me, or any athlete, having no idea what it's like, is just rude, rude, when you're listening to people talking about suicide, talking about mental health issues— and your response is this? Good on you mate.

Being a professional athlete is not a nine-to-five job, it's 24 hours a day until you reach a certain age or your body falls apart, and then it's nothing. There are a lot of sacrifices and it's hard, it really is. When it's over, it's over for good.

44

...

Harry

Being pregnant, I was sober and off all drugs and completely focused on something growing inside of me. Having miscarried before made me even more determined to do everything in my power to make sure this baby lived. I'd actually stopped all exercise, too, because I was still on bed rest after coming back from Seattle.

Becoming pregnant the first time I'd been really nervous but excited, I was so happy when I saw that first home pregnancy test, I still have it. I told my mum and she was so thrilled, we all were, but that's when I learnt pretty quickly that you don't tell people you're pregnant until much later. Losing that baby was devastating. It's a big shift in your brain from the thought of becoming a mum, to the realisation that the chance to be a mother, my baby was suddenly gone. I'd thought I was ready, but it wasn't to be. Being pregnant again felt like perfect timing, I was completely ready, I no longer had basketball commitments and all the associated travel, and would be wholly his or hers. Being an older mum I knew I'd appreciate my baby more than I would have in, say, my twenties, I don't know how I would have dealt with it back then, because I was focused wholly and solely on myself.

I didn't enjoy being pregnant, I was scared I was going to lose my baby the whole time, after that first miscarriage and then the haemorrhage in Seattle. Every day I'd wake up and check for a heartbeat—or just try and get the baby to kick when it was big enough—and just worry, all the time. That worry consumed me. Would I love the baby when it arrived? Would I cope? I almost talked myself into the fact that my baby wasn't going to make it, but I do that when I shouldn't. I had the usual ultrasounds you have when you're pregnant, and was always relieved every time I saw the little heartbeat flutter inside me. I didn't socialise much when I was pregnant. When I would go out I'd want to have a few drinks, so it was easier to stay at home—although the few times I did socialise I quite enjoyed being the designated driver, it had never happened before. Mostly, though, I really did just want to be alone.

Before falling pregnant I had to get X-rays of my hip and pubis area, and I actually saw the damage and the arthritis in that region after all the injuries I'd sustained over the years. My doctors had also seen the issues with my hip/pelvic area during routine scans on my hamstring, and had mentioned pinning it together post-retirement. Then I fell pregnant, and decided to wait, but there were times during my pregnancy that I couldn't get out of bed, I couldn't walk because of the pain there.

My blood pressure was high, and in January I was diagnosed with pre-eclampsia, a serious condition that can limit the blood supply to the baby, and so the doctors gave me a steroid injection to help mature the baby's lungs. Harry Gray Jackson arrived on 2 February 2017 at 11.44 am by caesarean section. He came a little early because of the pre-eclampsia, and when my little boy arrived he was so tiny. It was really strange, me being such a big human and having this tiny little 2.6 kilogram baby, he looked like a skinny little mouse, but he was so perfect. Mum was with me and she always reminds me that she was the first to see him.

I named him after my maternal grandfather Harry, who'd passed away when I was just 14 weeks old. My mum was so close to her dad, and I remember going to the cemetery to visit his grave with Mum all the time when I was a kid. He was always a presence in my life, even though I didn't know him. I wanted to also include Dad's name, but Harry Gary didn't work, so I transposed a couple of letters, and we have Harry Gray.

When Harry arrived, the adrenaline afterwards took me totally by surprise, I didn't go to sleep for 36 hours, all I could do was look at him and smile. I've never felt anything like that in my entire life, no matter how great a win was or a championship or a MVP, I'd never felt anything like what I experienced after he was born. I remember thinking after retiring that I'd never again experience that level of elation I'd felt when playing and winning, I thought that could never be reproduced. The euphoria I felt after giving birth to Harry was a little bit different, but not that much, and there was an additional level of intensity that I never had when I was playing. The chemical release and the adrenaline pumping through my body after the birth reminded me of those sporting highs, but this experience was so much better.

My baby boy turned out to be the most perfect thing that ever happened to me. Having Harry in my life now has highlighted to me what love should be, and I've never had that with anyone before. When you've had relationships and they fail constantly, the last thing you want to do is get into another one. I've never had a traditional live-in relationship, and I'm really fortunate that because of basketball I will never have to depend on another human being for anything, I'm so grateful for that. Having Harry, I've never been happier in all my life. I think I always knew that if I was going to have a child it would be on my own, and I don't regret anything, Harry is my pride and joy.

I'm a single parent but I'm not alone, I have my wonderful family and amazing friends. Sam, my old friend from Albury and my partner in crime in the Jameson evening in Spain is Harry's spiritual dad, and I can't think of a more honest man to help with Harry's upbringing. Katrina Hibbert and Sue Bird are his spiritual mums. He's going to have a lot of strong male role models around him, his grandfather, his uncle, his father, wonderful male friends of mine, who he'll learn a lot from. His father's also an important part of Harry's life, but out of respect for him I've chosen not to talk about him in this book.

Before having Harry, I could never imagine how Mum could get such pleasure out of watching me, and being there for me, I always thought it must have been hard for her, but now I want a child of mine to do a million times better than I ever did. I want him to be a good kid, respectful, a gentle young man. I suppose like all mothers, I just want my child to be healthy and happy.

I do want Harry to be a leader, not a follower, I want him not to feel pressured by his peers to be a certain way, not to go down the path of actively being a bully, saying hurtful things or being disrespectful. I will talk to Harry about social issues as he grows up, make him aware, and I'm going to ask him to be kind—to be kind and respectful of people.

If he's keen, Harry can play basketball. When he's young I will get him into sport because I think the lifestyle is the best way to go for kids, get them out of the house, away from in front of the television, in front of any sort of screen. So I think I'll get him into something, whatever he wants to do or enjoys doing, any sport, just for fun. Being my child, he'll be tall, and like my parents did for me, I'll encourage him to do what he wants to, what he can do.

No matter how well prepared you think you are for a baby and the demands of motherhood, I don't think you have any idea until you've actually had a child. They arrive and you're just thinking, there is my life gone. The first couple of weeks there were definitely times when I'd look at him and be frightened, thinking 'This is now my life', and it really scared me. That feeling didn't last too long, but I know that my life will never be the same, it's so much better.

45

...

Accident

Mum was a terrific help with Harry, and I don't know what I would have done without her in those first few weeks. I was getting back on my feet, juggling a baby and doing membership work with the Boomers, and she would regularly come and stay and help me out. Mum and Dad had made a decision that they would do whatever they could to help so that I didn't have to get a nanny because of work, and Mum was around a lot early on.

Harry was about four months old, and Mum had been with us in Albury, she'd come down for a day or two, before organising to meet up with Dad and then go to Sydney together, to celebrate their 40th wedding anniversary the following day. They had a nice hotel room booked, and were planning on staying four or five days away together. I drove Mum to Yass and met up with Dad, and we organised to see each other the following week, and I decided to go home via Junee to catch up with my brother Ross's family that night. Ross was away working in Thirlmere.

Harry and I arrived in Junee at about four in the afternoon, booked into a hotel room and got ready to meet Ross's wife Nicky and their two gorgeous kids, her sister and her parents, for dinner at six. As we were getting ready, I shared a couple of text messages with Mum, telling her we'd arrived and were looking forward to catching up with everyone. For some unknown reason I decided not to take my phone to the dinner and left it in my room. The first time I've ever done that.

We went to dinner, I met up with my sister-in-law, her kids and some of her family, when Ross called Nicky. Her face just dropped as she listened, and she was freaking out, I knew straight away in my gut that something bad had happened. She looked at me and I think she said there'd been an accident and put me on the phone to Ross.

Mum and Dad had been in a bad car accident, Mum had been trapped in the car and was severely injured and was being transported by ambulance to Canberra Hospital. Dad had been trying to call me, but when he couldn't reach me called Ross. I lost it, I'd already had a glass of wine, it was winter, dark outside and I knew I shouldn't drive on icy roads upset, but that night in the hotel room was the worst night of my life, not knowing how Mum would be. I've never felt that helpless before, I didn't know how bad her injuries truly were. I was calling the hospital every hour for updates until four in the morning, and at first light I packed Harry into the car and drove to Canberra.

Ross had driven straight to the hospital from work, and when we arrived we found Mum black and blue, with a massive cut to her head, multiple broken bones—it was shocking, I've never been so scared in all my life, seeing her so vulnerable and in so much pain. Harry was so good, we waited with Dad and stayed by her side. All the gratitude and love, everything I felt for my Mum, came to the surface like never before. My mother has done everything for me, emotionally, spiritually, physically, she has helped me every way that she can. She was everything to me, my best friend, my soul mate, everything, seeing her like that made me aware of her mortality and how quickly life can change.

She couldn't speak properly, was incoherent, and Dad filled me in. Mum had a fractured sternum, bruised ribs, her left leg was smashed, she had a fractured tibia and fibula (shin and calf bones), a fractured scaphoid (a bone in the wrist), and even her big toe was dislocated. She had internal bruising and a large gash on her head where she'd hit the windscreen.

Mum and Dad had driven home from Yass after I'd seen them, and were just outside Moruya when it happened, a road they'd been on just about every day since moving to the South Coast. A young male driver who'd been travelling in the opposite direction had swerved to miss a kangaroo, crossed over to the incorrect side of the road and hit Mum and

Dad head on. His Hilux hit the windscreen on the passenger side where Mum was sitting, became airborne after impact, and ended up down an embankment. It happened within a split second and there was nothing my parents could do, they took the impact head on.

Mum was in hospital for a few weeks. She had surgery on her leg, and a plastic surgeon fixed the gash on her face and head. Dad, Harry and I stayed at a hotel to start with and then with friends, until she was eventually transferred by ambulance to Moruya Hospital, where she stayed for another week. When I was at Moruya, I met one of the SES guys who'd cut her out of the car, who told me my mum was one tough woman. When they took her out, blood had been spurting out of her head, and her leg was badly damaged— he kept saying she was tough, so strong, and what an amazing woman I have in my mum. She's so strong, she's remarkable. The number of people she's impacted through her kindness and her strength really showed after the accident. Every day I was getting calls from people when they heard what had happened—even from my bank manager, who also deals with my mum, she actually started crying she was so upset. Mum has touched so many people with her kindness, she's such a beautiful, caring person.

I stayed with my parents after Mum was released from hospital, she wasn't walking and she needed help with everything. That time really strengthened my relationship with her. I'd always relied so heavily on her for everything, and now it was a complete role reversal. Cooking, cleaning, helping Dad out, we looked after her together. I've seen a part of my dad that's made me love and respect him even more, the way he's taken care of my mother is phenomenal, he would care for her, wash her, I'm so proud of him.

If that had all happened a year or two before I would have crumbled, I would have turned to every vice I had, but now I couldn't, I had Harry. I needed to make sure he was okay. It doesn't matter how horrible everything is, I can't focus on me like I used to. I need to focus on my boy, and sharing him with Mum, she got so much joy having him around in the first few months after the accident, it was really lovely, she adores her grandchildren.

Harry all through this time was such a beautiful baby, he knew something was wrong the night of the accident, he's such an old soul. I need to be well for him, he makes me a better person as a result. I hadn't realised until that accident that motherhood gives you a strength, and with that knowledge, I was able to take better care of my own mum. For the first few weeks we were with her at the hospital every day, Harry would lie on a mat on the floor in Mum's ward at the hospital, we just stayed there every single day.

It's taken Mum a long time to recover, and even as I write this, many months after the accident, she's still not walking by herself, having to rely on crutches and a scooter to get around, but she's getting better every time I see her. She's lost so much weight, and it's been horrible to see her go through it all. But it's made me appreciate her, both my parents, and I hold them and Harry a little tighter as a result.

46

...

From Here

Basketball gave me a lot to be thankful for, my friends, a career playing all over the world, and the experiences that came with that. It's a world sport, and not just three or four months out of the year, it's played year-round, across both hemispheres. I think people underestimate what basketballers do and how big the sport is worldwide, because here in Australia it's not as massive as overseas.

As a kid, playing basketball was its own sphere of happiness for me, everything else, whatever was happening outside of basketball didn't matter, because when I stepped on the court, I could go and let out whatever I was feeling and just play. The determination came as I grew, and it grew with me. My poor dad, he told me recently that he's felt bad ever since he told me to get back out on the court in the match before I wrote the mission statement, believing he's the reason that I played through pain the way I did throughout my career. That's not the case, I just grew up. It was my choice, I was going to play and be the best I could. I was determined, I played in the Sydney Olympics as I dreamt and aimed for, and went on further by pushing myself. It was my choice.

I was so young, and all of a sudden, I was in this life where you get whatever you want, do whatever you want, it was out of control, but when I was younger I lived for it. The more professional the sport, the more removed from life athletes can become. It's a form of isolation, almost. You have everything done for you so you can focus on bringing out the best in your body physically. I've heard comments from some of the general public whose view of athletes is that we're spoilt brats—but we're not. We've spent years and years aiming for one goal, to get our bodies as fit as humanly possible.

As a professional athlete, I was paid to do what I loved, but there were a lot of sacrifices that came with that, whether it was my physical, emotional or mental health, or just being away from my family and those I love.

Physically, all those years playing professional basketball year-round have taken a toll on my body, the aches and pains I have for my age—it's just ridiculous. But compared to the sort of pain I was in from 2012 to 2016, I'm fine. The nature of my injuries and all of those surgeries, I don't think I'll ever have to go through nearly as much pain as what I've already been through. I don't think I'm even aware of the constant ache happening in my body until I have to bend over to do something with Harry and it takes me about ten seconds to straighten back up, or I go to open a car door and my thumb pops out. Certain things like that are going to bother me, get to me, but after pushing myself from one extreme to another while managing pain, I know that I can cope. My other knee will eventually have to be looked at, probably sooner rather than later. I still have pins in my hips, shoulder, ankle and knee, but my Achilles is now great, and as long as I can walk, I'm good.

I look back and I do sometimes think I could have rehabbed my body better, taken more time between seasons to go to the AIS and get as strong as I could, but whenever I eventually did have a break I just wanted to be with my family at home, and I wanted to be with my friends, because I hardly ever saw them. That was my priority, and that's probably the only thing I look back on in my career and think, I could have done that better.

I'll always be a basketballer at heart, that will never go away. I was lucky to have as many years as I did, but towards the end the pain was enough to make me want to throw in the towel. I still have moments where I dream of being able to play again, jump and move, have that body again, be who I was.

Mentally, I had struggles throughout my career with anxiety and depression. I think my anxiety led on to the really horrible stuff, but I was fortunate that I never had to pretend to be anything other than who I was. Prescription drugs evened out the physical pain and depression, but as I got older the drugs became more and more powerful, in order for me just to get through each day.

Emotionally, I'm happy. That's an ever-changing state, and I think I've been through the worst, but then I had a child and apparently every day you worry. But it's a different worry—it's not that I don't care about myself anymore, because I do, but for now it's all about him. I'm grateful that basketball gave me the means to help support him, but I still have to work, and that's fine. I have my job with the Boomers, I'm passionate about it, I've become passionate about the team watching them play, and even the off-court side of it I'm really enjoying. I've also got a gig with Fox Sports commentating the WNBL for the 2017/2018 season, which is a lot of fun and definitely igniting my passion for the sport again—watching it through a different lens is giving my love of basketball a new lease of life.

The minute I retired, I wasn't an athlete anymore. When it's over, it's done, and normally you're a bit worse for wear physically. Emotionally, I'm lucky I came out better than when I was playing.

Looking back, I guess I didn't understand how big my achievements were at the time, I was just living each day as it came. With the highs and lows of the sport, combined with the depression, one day I would feel like I could achieve something really great, then the following day or week I would hit a low point so hard that it swept away all the good things happening at that time, and I'd focus instead on how bad I felt within myself. That all detracted from what I was achieving. I was so down, I hadn't found myself as a human being, it took away from an exciting time in my life.

I would have loved to have won an Olympic gold medal, it would have been awesome. It would have been amazing, but realistically, even though we did have very talented players in our national team, we just weren't at the level of the Americans. The US is the US. Athens was probably the closest we came to gold in my career. How do I feel about not winning gold? Is it my biggest regret? No. I don't look back and think that it's the worst thing that ever happened, because it wasn't. I had a great career, and a lot of fun with great people along the way. How can you regret that?

Of everything I experienced in basketball, it is all the good people who have come into my life, and those who have supported and loved me unconditionally, that I appreciate the most. My parents, my mum—the love and support they have given me over my life has been so complete. After their car accident, the possibility of losing my mum shook me to my core. I could never appreciate how much motherhood meant, the unreserved love you give to your child, the desire to see them happy, before I had Harry. I now have a whole new level of love and respect for both of my parents.

It's fair to say that since Harry arrived I have never felt more complete or content as an adult—don't get me wrong, there have been some real struggles, but having him here has made me aware that it isn't just about me anymore, it's about this beautiful little soul who I'm responsible for, and that alone motivates me to be the best version of myself I can be.

Basketball is a great sport, it let me experience the world, but my world now is Harry—and around that, having a career that can still incorporate my love of basketball, and figuring out the balancing act that is life. I still want to incorporate all the things I used to do with charities and speaking engagements, I have one last unit left to finish my degree—and that's interesting when combined with raising a child—but as with the rest of my life and loves, I'm figuring it out.

I've realised my dreams, been there for my teams, experienced so many highs and lows. The game of basketball, the game that has given me so much, is almost an analogy for my life. You take the hits, you get the ball, you score the buckets, you may miss occasionally, but you just play it to the best of your ability.

Major achievements

WNBL—Canberra Capitals
6 WNBL Championships
4 WNBL MVP
6 WNBL All-Star
4 Grand Final MVP

WNBA—Seattle Storm
2 WNBA Championships
3 WNBA MVP
8 WNBA All-Star

Europe
3 EuroLeague Championships
2-time EuroLeague All-Star
2 Russian Championships
1 Spanish Championship
1 EuroLeague Final Four MVP

Australia—Opals

3 Olympic silver medals

1 Olympic bronze medal

1 FIBA World Championship gold

2 FIBA World Championships bronze

1 Commonwealth Games gold